D0915377

THE SEA IS FOR SAILING

The Sea
is for Sailing

Peter Pye

John de Graff, Inc.

New York

1961

First published in Great Britain in 1957
First U.S.A. Edition 1961
© E. A. Pye, 1957

Lithoprinted in U.S.A.
EDWARDS BROTHERS, INC.
Ann Arbor, Michigan

ACKNOWLEDGMENTS

I would like to thank the Editors of the *Yachting World,
Yachting Monthly* and the *Royal Cruising Club Journal* for
their kind permission to reprint some of the material
which appeared originally in those magazines

CONTENTS

PHOTOGRAPHS

CHAPTER ONE

THE WHEEL OF FORTUNE

ANNE once said that we sail with one hand in God's pocket. I think we live our lives that way, too, for this story would never have been told if the long arm of coincidence had not sent the Smeetons striding down the sea wall at Farnbridge in Essex at the same time that it sent me up it.

The wind was from the north and there was snow in the air. Miles was six foot six, with a face whose form suggested that it had been sparingly carved from teak, a Roman nose and a look of the mountains in his stride; Beryl walked behind him. They were laughing as they hurried down the path, no overcoats, no scarves, no hats . . . the hairs on Miles's chest peeping through his half-buttoned shirt.

A few yards later I stopped in my tracks. There was something in the air. . . . With a prickly feeling running up my neck I turned and followed them down to the shed. Pausing a moment to think up an excuse for such unwarrantable curiosity, I opened the door and walked in.

Mick the boatman said, "Ah, here's Dr Pye. He might be able to help. He's just come back from the West Indies."

Miles looked down. "Pye . . . Pye . . . where have I heard that name? I know; you met a friend of mine, Dick Goss, at Tobago. He said if that man could cross the Atlantic in a boat like his, he was sure I could."

A most engaging smile spread over Miles's face, "I hope he's right," he said. "I am looking for a boat to sail back to British Columbia."

The Smeetons found *Tzu Hang* at Dover. She was a forty-five-foot ketch, built at Hong Kong of teak on the lines of *Tai-Mo-Shan*. They had never sailed before, but they took her across the Thames Estuary at night and made the entrance to the Crouch on the morning tide.

At that time we were settling into our cottage at Steeple, and often, when we went over to Burnham, Beryl would be swing-

ing at the masthead from a bos'n's chair. I remember her as a
small, brown person, as sure-footed as a mountain goat, a
woman who had walked across Turkestan, ventured alone into
Tibet, ridden up the Andes, and with Miles, reached 22,000
feet on Tirich Mir.

Whenever I think of Miles I remember a morning on the
Crouch when *Tzu Hang* and *Moonraker* were anchored side by
side. It was one of those slightly misty days, and Miles was
standing by the mast looking down the river to where the low
banks seemed to run into space, so that if you were to set sail
your course would take you at once into strange, uncharted seas.

"The world would be intolerable," he said, "if adventure
were not just around the corner."

One way and another we saw a good deal of the Smeetons
that spring. Clio came back from school. She was tall and thin,
a child of ten with a puckish face who was always reading
books. By the time they reached Victoria, Clio would have
lived in half the countries in the world and crossed a couple of
oceans.

I heard a grown-up say to her once, "How wonderful to
have had all those experiences," to which Clio replied in a
small serious voice, "I've had too many experiences."

Just before they left we were having dinner aboard. We
were talking about the Galapagos Islands and of the families
that inhabit those remote places, when Miles suddenly said,
"Why don't you come out to British Columbia and spend the
winter with us?"

On the way back to our cottage that night the smell of the
countryside, the fields and the view from Steeple Hill over the
River Blackwater, a ribbon in the moonlight, made the idea of
leaving it seem the most foolish thing we could do. We spoke
no words, but instead of going upstairs Anne pulled out an
atlas.

Atlases are no cure for pipe-dreams. With a hand-span you
can reach out half across the largest ocean, and the sea is a
delicate blue without a single wave.

Anne said, "Look; we can go to the South Sea Islands, up to
Hawaii and then to Victoria."

Her finger travelled down the west side of America.

"I've always wanted to go to Mexico, and then we can come back through the Panama Canal and the West Indies."

"That'll be fun, beating against the winter Trades."

She looked at me scornfully, "*Tai-Mo-Shan* did it, so why can't you?"

If you look at *Moonraker* with an unbiased eye (a thing neither Anne nor I can do) you will see a short-ended (one might almost say no-ended) cutter with great freeboard for'ard, very little aft, a tremendous sheer, high bulwarks, a transom stern and a long bowsprit. A ship that looks like a box and sails like a witch, built in the year 1896 by the eye of a craftsman, in a shape that might bring tears to the eyes of Mr. Jack Giles but would please those of Captain Joshua Slocum.

Twenty-nine feet long, drawing six feet and over and with a foot more beam than *Wanderer III*, she is built of pitch-pine planking on oak frames. She is a happy ship; sea-kindly and safe when running before a strong wind, capable of inspiring the utmost loyalty in all her crew. I suspect she is extremely jealous, for if ever Anne and I go sailing in another boat, she lets things fall off her or sails like a pig until we beg her forgiveness. If she thought we were going to sell her, she'd drown us.

Such was the ship that Anne and I left a year later as we rowed down the Fowey river to meet Christopher, our crew, at the station. It was pouring with rain.

Christopher had the same name as our previous crew; he was *x*, the unknown quantity. He was twenty; he had been to Eton, had sailed as a boy and mate in a Thames barge, had a commission in the Twelfth Lancers during his National Service, had spent a week of still autumn weather with us, had rung up from Switzerland to put off helping us to fit out the ship and was now coming straight from Henley. His father had said, "I'm sending him with you instead of to a university."

We loaded his kit-bag, his suitcase, his bowler hat and his gun into the pram and set off up the winding river. On the one hand a rather gorgeous young man in an exquisite reefer jacket, on the other, two oil-skinned figures with rivers of rain running off their crumpled sou'westers.

An idea came into my head.

"Have you got a dinner jacket in that case?" I asked.

"Yes, of course I have," he said.

CHAPTER TWO

TO PANAMA

CLOSE-HAULED to a fine north-westerly breeze we said good-bye to the shores of England early in July, gave Ushant a berth of thirty miles, nearly missed Spain by a gross navigational error, flew down the coast with a strong fair wind and, off the entrance to Camarinas, gybed to make into the bay.

There was a sudden crack up aloft. "Oh, look, Peter, look!" wailed Christopher. "There's something wrong."

There was indeed. The gaff had broken off at the gooseneck and Anne and I clawed down the sail.

Christopher stopped biting his nails. "If that had happened outside," he said, "I suppose we'd have had it."

"Not at all," said Anne equably, "you would have mended it."

We had come this way before when coming to Barbados in 1949. Then we had sailed through the West Indies by way of Bermuda. This time we planned to revisit English Harbour in Antigua before going through the Panama Canal and for this reason we didn't linger on the Spanish coast.

Our last port of call in Spain was Bayona. We had not meant to stay there for more than a night, but Anne and Christopher were ashore shopping when a Spaniard, in a rich Scottish accent, asked whether he could help with a little interpreting.

Miguel became our friend. He showed us where to eat oysters by the hour instead of by the dozen, he took us up a mountain to the remains of a pre-Roman village, the foundations of each little round dwelling still standing with a place for the pole to keep up the thatched roof, and to a restaurant overlooking the Minho which divides Spain from Portugal.

Over the very river above which we were now sitting he had, during the war, helped to smuggle Allied airmen until a friend at the Foreign Office warned him that he had been discovered and unless he left the country within forty-eight hours he would most certainly be put in prison.

His wedding was in two days' time. "But," said Miguel, pointing down the hill to an inconspicuous barn, "I spent a very pleasant honeymoon, waiting for a moonless night."

His escape to England was uneventful, and as he was a doctor of some note in his own country he was given a post at a famous London hospital. After the war he returned to Spain and became the leading specialist in his own line.

One day an influential acquaintance of his asked him to take a young man on as his assistant. A year or two later this young man told Miguel that he was engaged to be married.

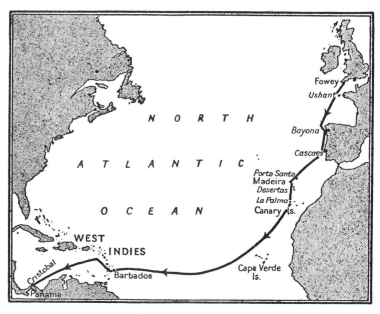

Fowey to Panama

"Splendid," said Miguel. "Who are you marrying?" The young man mentioned an illustrious name.

"I do indeed congratulate you. I suppose, now that your work will be more political than medical, you will be giving up your appointment here?"

The young man smiled at him thinly. "I shall be giving up my post," he agreed. "I have been given yours."

Cascaes, 320 miles to the south, lies at the entrance to the Tagus. We ghosted in, the genoa and topsail doing all the work. A voice, made raucous by the loud hailer, called, "Would the English boat with the red sails now entering the harbour please keep outside the racing marks?"

That is the trouble with Portugal. The fishermen and the peasants are much like their Spanish neighbours, a little more dour, perhaps, and much more ironic; but this place, for all its Moorish look, the hills of Sintra and the rakish trawlers with their high, flared bows, might almost as well be Cowes.

Among the fleet of chromium-plated yachts, tucked away in a quiet corner, were three craft of a different sort. The *Viking*, a double-ended Swedish boat, was a bermudian ketch. Sten and Brita Homdahl, blond and strong, had made their small cabin themselves. It smelt of pine woods, and above the stove was a painting of a little house in the forest, all covered with snow. I hoped it would keep them cool in the tropics.

Behind the *Viking* was *Wanderer III*, as English as her crew, so workmanlike, so dependable that the success of their voyage round the world was as much a foregone conclusion (to us if not to them) as a passage from Southampton to Cherbourg in the *Queen Mary*.

The third ship was the *Harry*.

The *Harry* was a Morecambe Bay prawner now owned by a Dutchman who, with a fellow countryman, was bound for San Francisco. He had a touching faith in his ship. He said, "She is much older and more versed in the ways of the sea than I. She can find her own way across the Atlantic."

I agreed that she might be older and even wiser, but was it fair to ask her to find an island ten miles long, three thousand miles away, without so much as an astrolabe?

"Ah," replied her skipper, "I may have no sextant, but I have four compasses."

Now in case any would-be voyager should think this a sensible thing to do, I will tell you what happened. They set out from one of the Canary Islands bound for Barbados but the *Harry* ran ashore on a beach in Brazil!

Viking, *Wanderer III* and ourselves were bound for the

Madeiras and La Palma but I had met a man in Funchal who had been to the Salvages, a deserted group of rocks only visited by fishermen.

He said, "They're more like the Galapagos than anything this side of the Pacific." He added, "Don't run on a reef, there's no water."

A hundred miles from anywhere! The web was spun.

On the way we ran into a patch of bad weather and for the first time the third reef was tucked into the mainsail.

There was a bit of a sea running and the wind was dead astern. Christopher took over from Anne at ten o'clock that night, and I pottered about the deck inspecting gear and watching Christopher's face peering anxiously into the binnacle and eyeing the lifting boom.

"All right?" I asked.

"Y-es, I think so."

I went below and slept with one ear open.

At the change of watch he called me. The look of strain had gone.

"Twenty miles on the log," he said. "Jolly good show!"

Porto Santo and Madeira, a night in the Ilhas Desertas: the ship sailed south. . . .

An island of laval rock mounting to a peak, a hollow bay with steep sides like a cavern, seas breaking green over a shelf, cries of shearwaters, thin and weak, shouts of wild-looking men, a longboat rolling in the swell; Anne's cry, "Less than three fathoms," paying out the chain till the anchor held, that is what entering the Ensenda de Cangarras on Selvagem Grande was like, just as darkness fell.

"A tierra. . . !" shouted the wild men. We obeyed.

Thick Porto Santo vowels echoing round the walls, barrels on the rocks, the hoarse commands of Paulo de Caries (a Rudolf Valentino, bearded and in rags), the stink of fish, the cauldron of soup bubbling on the brazier, flares lighting up the caves where men lived among the rats.

This was their last night here. Their water catchment was empty, the last shearwaters were being rammed into the last barrels, the long staves with their barbs for hooking the birds out of their holes were being stacked in the caves, and by this time tomorrow the island would no longer ring to the cries of men for many months to come.

Loaded down with three eggs, a present from their meagre store, the back end of a tunny fish and twelve salted shear-waters, none of which we dared to refuse, we departed. For two nights we ate those birds . . . a cross between a duck and a sardine and far, far richer than either. I was on watch. Ahead were lights that were half-way up a mountain on La Palma thirty miles away. There were six shearwaters left. Making sure that Anne was sound asleep, I dropped them overboard.

La Palma stands like a sentry looking over the Atlantic Ocean, and, like all sentries, it seems very much alone. Its people are tough and independent, poor and proud. A thousand feet above the little town is a church built in 1704. Around the walls are silver ships presented by princely merchants in thanksgiving to God for saving their lives, lanterns of ship-wrecked vessels, paintings of heroic deeds at sea. We look down over terraces of vineyards, orange trees with round, bright fruit and in the distance Pico de Tenerife rises out of the sea like a benevolent Mount Everest.

We get to know the shape of that mountain well for we are in sight of it for three days after leaving Santa Cruz de La Palma. From La Palma to Barbados is a distance of two thousand seven hundred miles. We pick up the Trades in 24° N. and sail within a hundred miles of the Cape Verdes.

A ship is a little world. Ours contains three people. Out of the hatch, overheated by oven and tropic sun bursts the mate with a sudden cry, "The damn' bread won't rise," and rushes to sit on the foredeck under the swelling sails.

Christopher pokes out a hopeful head, "Should my inter-cept be nearer the sun, or farther away?", sighs, and goes back to his plotting.

Washing your face in an inch of water, feeling the salt in your flying hair, the warmth of the sun through an ancient shirt, turning out in the night to silence a tin that rolls with the rolling ship, seeing the same faces from four feet across the cabin sole day after day, week after week, if these things don't

2

seem worth while, give up your dream of the southern seas and take Mr Weston Martyr's advice and catch the nine-fifteen.

The ship sails on under her Trade Wind rig. The swoop of the frigate bird, the flash of dolphin, the scatter of flying-fish, taking the ship's position, comparing the last day's run, the smell of coffee brewing, landfall after twenty-eight days.

Barbados lies ahead. We round Needham Point and the day and the wind go out like a light. *Moonraker* pauses reluctant to leave the peace of the ocean for the worries of the land. A boat puts out from the bay.

Breathless as if he had been rowing a race, Sten clutches our bulwarks: "How many days? How many days? Today we too come in."

The customs has come and gone, our friend has rowed back to his ship. Christopher has already turned in and Anne is making our bed. The green light of a schooner stealing into the bay, the ragged sail of a fishing boat caught in the gleam of the riding light,

> Up in the mornin', out on the job,
> Work like the devil fo' me pay,
> While tha' lucky ol' sun has nothin' to do
> But roam about heav'n all day.

The West Indies—again.

Christopher has jaundice in Barbados, I at English Harbour. I fret over the weeks of delay, and it is not until towards the end of January that we set sail for the Panama Canal. We take a slight risk letting her sail herself at night in these waters. I see a steamer alter course having seen our sails in the moonlight. I sleep better for this.

It is a curious thing that each of us goes up at least twice every night, and yet none of us meet: a subconscious watchkeeping, or a deep-rooted instinct for self-preservation.

The winter Trade Winds blew freshly, the spinnakers strained at their poles like greyhounds on the leash, but I was desperately weary and very glad when we sighted the light on Isola Grande at ten o'clock one night. The aerial beacons, the loom of lights contrasted strangely with the savage jungle half seen beneath the moon.

Relaxed and pleased as I always am when the ship swings to her anchor, I found that a busy day lay in front of us. Being measured for the canal, forms, questions, answers and a long row to the Port Captain's Office without delay. A pleasant young man, the Measurer, said, "We'll give you a pluck in there."

"It'll cost 'em seven bucks," growled his chief.

We rowed.

The Zone at Cristobal is a narrow strip of land running along the waterside between it and the Panama Railway. In it are the offices, clubs, commissaries and houses belonging to the Company. The houses are mostly two-storied frame buildings all very much alike with only a lick of paint and the termites holding hands to keep them up. On the other side of the railway lies the Panamanian town of Colon, a place of mean streets, of rather ugly houses; an unfortunate town, we felt, because it is too near civilization to drift into the slovenliness which seems its natural bent. A nearness that gives it traffic lights, drugstores and Bay Street where passengers from "cruise ships" buy Guatemala homespuns and Hindu curios.

But if, after a little while in the Zone, you get tired of seeing too many large and open-hearted men, so alike that you have to look twice to recognize your friends, too many well-turned-out women wearing the same sort of clothes, shoes and lipstick, all tanned to the same shade of brown, their shapely heads shown to the best advantage by the newest style of haircut, then cross the line and rest the eye upon a motley scene of many colours, blacks, whites and yellows, some fat, some thin, some with slanting eyes, others with eyes that sparkle with life, faces creased with laughter, faces sullen, faces kind and faces cruel; but different, as different one from the other as their cousins across the railway are alike.

The Yacht Club is a ramshackle looking place with a restaurant, hot and cold showers and a bar which is rarely empty. Scattered around are various sheds, a patch of grass where sails can be laid out to dry, a slip for vessels drawing six feet or less and a large open building in which members build their own boats.

Outside is a notice which reads:

This space is reserved for Naval Architects and their critics.

A casual "Hi-ya" or "Hallo" may come your way; then someone comes along and looks at your boat and steps aboard for a drink. Very soon he is telling you that he, too, is going to the South Sea Islands, only he came in a year ago meaning to stay a week. But the Zone is short of men, the pay is good and his pal landed a job before the week was up and as he couldn't go on alone he got a job too. Then he met a girl and the months slipped by and the worm got into his ship. Presently he takes you along and shows you what had once been a live and sentient thing, a ship of grace and beauty with a few bits of running gear hanging from her masts and that dusty look that ships, like women, get when they are no longer cared for.

You walk back with him to your own ship more determined than ever not to let her stay here too long. He puts his hand on your shoulder, for by now you are on intimate terms, and says, "Say, Peter, you don't want a crew, do you? It's time I got out of this joint."

You explain that you haven't got room for a fourth, and then you realize he never thought for one moment you would. It was a gesture . . . and he strolls back to the Club and goes into the bar for a whisky.

After a few days the place starts to grow on you. People help you to store up the ship, they drive you around and it is pleasant, after the drenching heat of the day, to sit on the Club veranda in the cool of the evening.

Someone says to Anne. "You can't go next week; we have friends coming in from Nassau, and I want you to meet with them."

And you say to yourself. "Why not do some of the work which has been so long postponed and stay here a little longer."

On just such an evening a big man with a square head and fleshy face came over to our table. Pointing to *Moonraker* he barked, "That yours?" We admitted it. He held out a large and flabby hand; "Name's Sam Brown, Assistant Port Captin. . . . Glad to know you, folks, and if there's anything I can do, I'm your man." We thanked him and I explained our lack of power and the awkwardness of our nine-foot bowsprit.

"For goodness sakes," he roared. "We'll have to tow you through behind a banana-boat. Against the rules, but rules don't matter to me. I'm retiring this year." Then he added, "What day d'you go through?"

"On Thursday!" I cried, at random.

The walls of the Gatun locks frowned down upon us from an immense height. We looked to our lines and fenders. The gates shut, and in a moment the whole placid surface of the water became a boiling cauldron. *Moonraker* surged and heeled and groaned but the *Real* (our banana-boat) took all the knocks against the wall and we came up, unscathed. Three times this happened, and then from a great height we looked our last upon the Atlantic and set off, with Captain Wilder, our pilot, across Gatun Lake.

Across wide spaces of rain-swept water, through narrow, swampy cuts, close to islands where alligators swam, the *Real's* diesel thumped its monotonous note. We slowed through the Gaillard Cut where, if she gets too close, the muddy bank may slew a big ship's stern round (and ruin the pilot); we were lowered a little at Pedro Miguel, crossed the Miraflores Lake to enter the locks which dropped us down to the sea. There is not much that is cheap left in the world of today but our transit, tow, pilot (paid £3,000 a year) and two long stalks of bananas, a present from the skipper of the banana-boat, cost five dollars and fifty cents.

At the watershed the rain had ceased and now, as the last great gates opened we saw for the first time the Pacific, shimmering like an inland lake in the afternoon sun.

CHAPTER THREE

FORBIDDEN ISLANDS

AMERICAN yachtsmen have a word for the Pacific; they call it "The Mean Sea". Islands disappear, new ones arise, tidal waves, tornadoes and waterspouts range across its waters like wolves over the Siberian plains. It is a vast sea, covering a third of the world and from here to the Marquesas, the first of the South Sea Islands, is not much more than half-way. Between Panama and the Marquesas are the Galapagos (Spanish for freshwater tortoise), islands that have been surrounded by mystery and on which strange things happen. They belong to Ecuador and we had been told that it would take more dollars and more time to get a visa than we could willingly spare.

"Don't go there without permission," said Captain Baverstock. "Yachts have been impounded and some have never been seen again."

The battle for our visa began next morning. I was told to be at the Consulate at ten o'clock. After waiting several hours I met the Consul. He was a short, dapper little man with an olive skin, faintly tinged with yellow. His English was much on a level with my Spanish but I understood I could have a visa for thirty dollars.

"How long will it take?"

"A month, perhaps."

I shook my head. The Consul said, "If you pay me fifteen dollars I send a cable to Quito."

"How long will that take?"

He shrugged his shoulders, "A week, perhaps."

We parted with expressions of mutual esteem.

That evening, two things happened. We met Señora de Sosa who had a friend in the Foreign Office, and we met Lee and Ann Gregg of the ketch *Novia*, bound for the Galapagos. So far, Lee said, his visa had cost him sixty dollars. He had applied for it three weeks ago, paid the fifteen dollars for the cable to Quito, but after a fortnight there was still no visa. So he had rung up the State Department in Washington, paid for them to ring up Quito and now, after paying another fifteen dollars to the Consul, he was expecting his visa on Thursday, the day before he sailed.

I went to the appointment with the friend in the Foreign Office, and after the week-end lull I returned to the Consul. He was more affable. A cable had been sent to Quito, my visa would cost me twenty dollars and no extras.

I was profuse in my thanks.

"When shall I get the visa?" I asked.

He shrugged his shoulders, "Perhaps Thursday, but if not I regret I am called away for a week."

The day before we left the anchorage frizzled under a burning heat, unrelieved by the usual Trade Wind. Inside air-conditioned offices (where I spent a good part of the day) it was pleasant enough, but as I sallied forth the heat hit the back of my neck like a sledgehammer and I arrived back on board peevish and thirsty.

There was no sign of tea. In a scattered heap on either bunk were seventy pounds of flour, cartons of cigarettes, cereals, wire trace, fish hooks and copper nails, while Christopher was cutting up a yard of bacon and Anne was stowing a mountain of fruit into boxes that I feared would be stowed on the cabin floor. The sweat dripping from their faces made me thirstier than ever, but it occurred to me that this was the moment to make myself as inconspicuous as possible. Delicately, like Agag, I abstracted a ball of marline from under a pile of toilet rolls and disappeared up the mast to reseize a thimble.

We dined that night with Señora de Sosa. We sat in a court-yard, open to the stars, in which palm trees and tropical plants in tubs and green things hung down from a balcony above. The house, nearly three hundred years old, stood four square about the courtyard, and the thickness of the stone of which it was built kept out the noise and stress of the city. We dined on Panamanian food at a Spanish hour and drank a Chilean wine. Towards the end of the meal one of the guests, the Chief of the Canal Personnel, said he thought that in ten years many

of the executive posts in the canal would be held by Pana-
manians.

Señora de Sosa, who had been talking to me about Ecuador,
broke off to flash a smile at him.

"Dear John," she said. "In ten years' time, there won't be
any of you left at all."

Next morning I went ashore to ring up the Ecuadorian
Consulate. At the head of the long concrete pier I met Ann
Gregg of the *Novia* sitting on a couple of wooden cases.

"Has Lee got his visa?" I asked.

She nodded. Ann is a dark, neat little person with, I should
have said, some Spanish in her blood, but this morning her
usually animated face looked vexed and worried.

Suddenly she burst into tears.

"I don't care who knows it . . . I'm just plain scared of
this goddam ocean, and if Lee doesn't come soon he'll find
me gone."

I knew so well how she felt, and I remembered having to
comfort Anne for hours, only that was a long time ago. So I
told her this, and how, one evening when I was rowing the late
Admiral Goldsmith (surely one of our most joyous small-boat
voyagers) back to his ship in Dartmouth, he suddenly leant
towards me and in a stage whisper that must have carried miles:

"I say, old boy," he said, "d'you ever get frightened when
you put to sea?"

"Every time, sir," I said.

"So do I, old boy—so do I!"

I saw Lee put off from his ship and when it no longer looked
as if Ann would run away, I went about my telephoning.

There was, of course, no visa.

I rang Señora de Sosa to thank her for our delightful evening.

"Did you get your visa?"

I told her we had not.

"You are going without?"

There was, although I may have been mistaken, a challenge
in her voice and I, having almost made up my mind to miss the
islands out, replied, "Of course."

Moonraker of Fowey

Skipper and Mate

Will Christopher pad about the streets in bare feet and bowler hat?

The last shear-
waters are put
into the last

When I got back to the ship she was ready for sea. The topsail had been bent on to the yard, and I noticed that she was lower in the water than she had ever been before. The only thing my crew had left for me to do was to sort the charts, and in case I should forget this they had placed them in a pile, with Chart No. 786 on top. This chart, from Cabo Corrientes to Cape Horn, displays a largish slice of the world. In the upper half is the great bight between Cabo Corrientes in Mexico to Punta Ajuta in Ecuador (a distance of 2,160 miles) at the head of which lies the Gulf of Panama looking, on this small scale, like an off-shore anchorage. The sea enclosed within this bight is notorious for its calms.

As I looked at this I thought of the Fisks whom we had met on our voyage to the West Indies. Now Pat, when I last saw him, had every intention of following the golden rule (for sailing ships) of making south to the Equator before sailing west to the Galapagos. But I think the people here, unused to English boats that rely on sail instead of power, must have persuaded him (as they tried to persuade me) to make straight to the islands. To give himself a greater range Pat lashed two extra drums of petrol on deck.

The Fisks carried a moderate wind out of the Gulf, and for one more day they were able to sail. Then it fell calm. Day followed day without a catspaw of wind to ruffle the surface of this silent sea and even the swell went down.

Pat motored on until, with his drums of petrol empty and his tank almost dry he had to stop his engine. The ship, like that of the ancient mariner, lay motionless on the painted ocean. The Humboldt current, welling up from the stormy wastes around the Horn, began to carry them north-westwards of the islands, and light airs pushed them slowly and inexorably into the counter-equatorial current which, clasping the ample *Debonair* in a fast embrace, took her backwards towards the American continent from which, with so much labour, she had just come.

While the children played with chalks on the cabin floor Pat and Maureen scraped and varnished to prevent themselves thinking of the future. They rationed water, but as Maureen said, it was difficult to tell children of four and six, when they were thirsty, that they must not drink.

For fourteen days they drifted backwards. Then Providence, not for the first time, intervened and as if to emphasize its bounty, sent them a black squall from the north-east in the middle of the night, almost dismasting them! Slowly, for other squalls followed, they worked their way southwards and, thanking God, they picked up the South-East Trades, driving their ship across three thousand miles of ocean to race their rapidly diminishing water supply. By the time they sighted the mountains of Hiva Oa in the Marquesas, one tank only held two gallons.

Remembering this, I saw that in the broad sea between the mainland and the Galapagos there was only a lane, a relatively narrow one, down which a sailor could steer his ship. If he strayed to the left he would run into the current coming up from the south, if to the right the same fate that overtook Pat might overtake him. Three hundred miles off the coast of Ecuador lay the islet of Malpelo standing like a signpost in the middle of the lane. For that island I should have to steer.

With Pat's story and that of the sailing ship that went round and round in the middle of the Gulf until her planking rotted and she fell apart, we sailed out into this strange sea, and before night was upon us it blew like smoke! That, of course, is a relative term, but it blew hard enough for me to take the topsail down, for Anne to mutter at me for not putting a reef in our brand new light-weight mainsail, and for the boom guy to part in the middle of the night causing her to gybe all standing and carry away the after runner cleat.

Christopher and I, arriving simultaneously on deck, disentangled Anne from the mainsheet which had nearly carried her overboard, hove-to and pulled down that reef. By noon we had sailed right out of the Gulf, a hundred and twenty miles in twenty hours.

On the morning we sighted Malpelo we were virtually becalmed. This lonely rock, covered with bird droppings and without a vestige of scrub on its rounded sides, looked very much like a sketch that Anne made of it; the head between

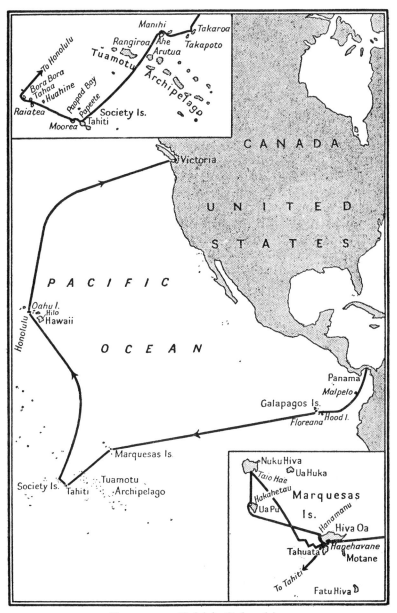

Panama to British Columbia

the paws, the arched back, the tail (a group of rocks) . . .
Pluto, to the life.

As the short twilight faded into night the air was filled with
the beat of wings and a thousand birds flew in low above the
water to their roost, and at that moment the gurgle round the
stem, the creaking of the blocks as they took the strain and the
curving of the sails proclaimed a breeze. That breeze became
our friend; it rose and fell, backed and veered, but not for a
moment did it leave us. Each night the Pole Star crept lower
in the sky, the Southern Cross rose higher, and then one morning we breakfasted in mid-winter and lunched in summer. That
night the Plough was upside down. We had crossed the line.

But we were anything but idle. Anne wrote, "Peter and
Christopher spend most of the day sail changing", and "I was
hot and sticky on watch but there was no peace for me as I
had to gybe three times. There is so little wind I would haul in
the sails and let us sleep but Peter says no———"

A few nights later, in a different mood, she wrote, "the
moon is up, catching a gleam from the varnish of the boom,
playing chequers on sails and spars, a night of tropic beauty.
As I see it, we are in the late afternoon of life. It has been a
long morning. In the cool hours, the growing up, the studying,
the fun of being young and keen and gay; then, as the sun rose
we settled down to work, to build a practice and to watch it
grow. In the afternoon we set off to sail the waters of the
world and see what we had been missing, shut up in our suburb.
All the hours are good if we do not grow too tired, too soon."

At dawn on the eleventh morning out from Panama we
came out of a rain squall to see a green island of middle height
fine on the port bow. The island is uninhabited, although two
wireless masts, relics of the American station built there during
the war, make us hesitate for a moment before anchoring in
Gardner Bay on Hood Island. It is covered with a thick green
scrub and cactus from which grows a yellowish sort of fruit.
Up the coral beach the sea rushes in long fan-shaped curves,
and in the cool green water, clear as crystal, are the bronze
shapes of sharks. The sea is alive with them, and we nose our
pram into the water gingerly. They take no notice and, gain-

ing courage, we row off to the beach, but I am *very* careful to choose the right wave to carry us in; nor do we waste any time in dragging the pram up the fine white sand. The island has been silent, but now the air is filled with the barking of sea-lions (oddly human in this deserted place), and black heads come swimming towards us. They land, bark genially, rub themselves in the sand and bathe in the surf. We bathe too but keep a wary eye open for sharks.

There is, we think, no water on this island. A flightless cormorant with a red bill follows Anne about like a tiny dog, pelicans swoop into the water after fish, red crabs spreadeagle themselves on black rocks, and a flock of black iguanas, under the charge of a large green one hurry away at our approach. The green one turns on us balefully. His scaly back and rudimentary spines suggest a resemblance to a prehistoric monster.

Floreana, thirty-seven miles to the west of Hood Island, is bigger and higher, having a mountain, an extinct volcano, of seventeen hundred feet. After the first war the Wittmers and the Ritters came out from Germany to settle here, the Ritters having first had all their teeth extracted and one pair of false teeth made out of steel which they wore on alternate days. Both the farms were in a valley on the west side of the island, they grew fruit, coffee beans and vegetables, and they never ran short of meat, for wild cattle roamed the island, left from some previous occupation.

Into this seemingly idyllic existence came the Baroness and her lovers and all the passions of a Grand Guignol unfolded on this remote island. One day this South Sea bubble burst; Ritter was found murdered, the Baroness escaped with some of her lovers in a boat which was eventually found on a neighbouring island. Their bodies were never identified.

It was off the north coast of this island that we found ourselves at dawn. A breeze, a gift of the early morning, hurried us along past age-old cliffs, grey and black, past Onslow Island whose centre had fallen in to make a small lagoon and around whose perimeter cacti stood like skeletons. We stood in to Post Office Bay.

No longer do outward bound sailing ships put in to post

letters in the barrel on the beach for other ships home from the whaling grounds to take back to the mainland, but less than a year ago a yacht came in for a day on passage from Holland to Tahiti. She had as crew a Dutchman, a Belgian and a German and her master, also Dutch, had the reputation of being a driver of men. Already Lamberty had had trouble with the German and the Belgian, and against his better judgment he put in so that these two could pay a visit to the Wittmers.

He said, "If you are not back by sunset, I sail without you."

The two men walked up to the Wittmers' farm, five miles and a thousand feet up, found the Wittmers out, removed some of their possessions (as souvenirs, they said) and returned to Post Office Bay. On the beach was a bundle containing their clothes and papers, but the ship had gone! They wrote letters in four languages begging the next ship to sail round to Black Beach and rescue them, put them into the barrel and started off on the long trail up to the farm only to meet the outraged Wittmers coming down.

We found the barrel on its side in a clearing behind the beach; empty. On the rotting post were nailed boards with the names of ships, the most recent being *Tzu Hang*, to which we added *Moonraker*, posted three letters in the box with money for stamps (all arrived a few months later) and rowed back to the ship. The only sound was the braying of wild donkeys.

There were soldiers, we had been told, at Black Beach, in the charge of a sergeant. I was unwilling to risk any chance of having the ship impounded; Anne said it was ridiculous to suppose they wouldn't let us call in for water, even if they didn't allow us to land, and Christopher backed her up, so we bearded Black Beach.

After mistaking a rock for a man-o'-war (so jittery was this Gilbertian crew), we arrived to find the soldiers had gone, the wireless station had not functioned for two years, and the Port Captain most amiable as long as we stayed only for a short time. We had missed the Government boat by two days!

It so happened that the Wittmer family were down at the beach in their little two-storied house they had built in three days from wood brought over from Seymour Island (ex-

U.S.A. base) by Irving Johnson in the brigantine *Yankee*. Of the four Frau Wittmer was the only one who could speak English. They let us fill up our tanks from their water catchment, gave us bananas and pineapples; we had supper with them and they accepted the small things we had brought them most graciously. It was so like calling on someone in a distant suburb, an event of so little importance in their lives, that it made me realize how completely self-contained you become if you live in a place where it takes a year and a day for a book to come from London by air mail.

We were just turning in that night when I thought I heard the creak of an oar very close to the ship. A bearded figure rose as if from the surface of the water, so loaded down was the dory in which he and his companion stood. In a voice so soft that it might have sprung from the Hebrides, he said, "Buenas noches, señor. ¿Quiere estas naranjas?"

While Christopher and I heaved three sacks, made of hide and full of firm green fruit, on to the deck, they and Anne settled down in an unhurried, tribal way to barter. Eleazer Cruz had bought the Ritters' farm which, being lower, produces fruit earlier than the Wittmers'. He had learned that a ship had come in from the mainland and needed oranges, so he picked all he could, loaded them on to a mule and had come down to look for the ship. When he saw *Moonraker* he almost turned back again, for how could such a cockleshell need so much fruit? When Anne explained that we should be at sea for a month he became most anxious. He was a man of the mountains and the valleys, he said, but he hoped, and I could see he thought it almost too much to ask, that God would watch over us. In the meantime there were things he would like to have for his children in exchange.

Anne, explaining carefully that in such a small boat our resources were very limited, offered him two cartons of cigarettes, three tins of porridge (a great delicacy this) and, best of all, a jar of bacon fat that our visitor saw standing in the galley.

The deal was confirmed over a glass of aguardiente and they clambered back into their dory and paddled silently away until their shadows were lost against those of the land.

CHAPTER FOUR

ACROSS THE PACIFIC

From Floreana to Hiva Oa in the Marquesas is 3,180 miles as we sailed it. As Anne saw it, it was thirty-eight days:

1st day. New baked bread from the Wittmers and a hot cooked lobster. Handkerchiefs flutter from the house with the narrow, lidded eyes. The sea before us is a vast heaving field of sparkling blue, the furrows many ships' lengths apart, and it looks as if it had no more land to offer.

2nd day. The little awning is rigged to make a tent for the helmsman. A short square whale sleeps with a little fountain spraying as he breathes. A red moon rises. I hang the Southern Cross in the port ratlines and the Plough upside down on the starboard quarter.

3rd day. The log line entangles in the night so fishing is frowned on. Galapagos tree tomato chopped as a flavouring is scented like juniper.

4th day. A hot ship, a glassy sea. The air is wet.

5th day. Hot, long, windless. The four-days'-old cake has a bloom of mould over it.

6th day. A sea of lumps and hollows. We fall and pound. We are right under the sun, and the sun's angle is 92 and cannot be subtracted from 90. After fruitless thought by us all C. suggests shooting from the east instead of the west. It is then too late.

7th day. Morning comes with a bang! All hands! *Moonraker* tries to push her way *through* the waves. C. is too asleep to tell topsail halyard from spinnaker. The breeze changes its mind a dozen times and we return to the rig we started with until tea-time when a North Sea mist and rain makes me suggest less sail, so Peter sends me below to make a fresh fruit salad and takes the helm till he fills the cockpit, floods the engine room (the porthole wide open) and decides to take in sail. Wet sails, wet crew, wet rugs. Rain. We rig the twins.

8th day. Tumbly seas, rain and squalls. I notice how large Christopher is. He shuts out the light.

9th day. Lustreless; when the after guy parts and the port boom leaps forward Christopher, shaking himself like a shaggy dog in the afternoon sun, wakes and says, "Can I help?" This makes Peter laugh. Little holes appear in the sails.

10th day. The spinnaker boom is lost as no one bothered to lash it on

The barrel at Post Office Bay

deck when changing to fore and aft rig. We hunt for it from dawn till lunch-time. Wretched day.

11*th day*. No comment.

12*th day*. Another reef earing gives. Peter burns his foot against the hot kettle, stubs his toe under the bulwark. He thinks he has broken it. A strand parted in a shroud lanyard. We heave to on the other tack and I hold the light while the others renew the lanyard using the after-runner tackle to bowse it down tight. The wind moans; they are up to their knees in water. The weather is bewitched; as fast as the eye can turn from compass to sky a squall is on us, from the side, the back and even from above. The wind and water hiss; stars are blotted out.

13*th day*. Fish jump and flying-fish fly. I am weary and lunch is of old biscuit. The sunset is a flood of amber beauty, and we let the ship sail herself all night with the foresail a little backed.

14*th day*. Sleep was wonderful, the day a delight. Porpoises snort and sharks glitter. Peter fits a new nipple to the Primus and cleans the galley while I bake bread and scone. Christopher renews a line on the gaff and greases the jaws. The potato locker is in his charge and he has not sorted it and half are rotten. I see a dirty ship, neglected gear, greasy topsides, unsorted onions, unwashed clothes and all of us lethargic. I say so. Peter snaps, C. is silent and I sulk.

15*th day*. The main halyard gives and a new one is rove. Peter sorts the onions and C. says, "Jolly good show." There is a quiet sky but an enormous sun halo. Steering is quiet peace.

16*th day*. The sun is warm. Christopher cleans the fo'c'sle and splices a new spinnaker sheet. Peter makes a complicated strop so that we can use the topsail yard for a spinnaker boom. There is a new young moon.

17*th day*. We go back to twins. Half the new rope is rotten with lying in the locker (in spite of airing it in port).

18*th day*. I darn the little holes in the mainsail and *Moonie* does her best to roll me off. Tonight we are rested; only 1,490 miles to go.

19*th day*. I feel stiff and sick. Peter wants something different to eat and has lost his pen and a screw from the mirror rolls into the bilge.

20*th day*. Blue sea and a smoky sky and a white bird hovers. I bake a good loaf at last! It takes $2\frac{3}{4}$ hours. I think of Liverpool Street Station and the London tube and the blue waves rolling along look good. Chicken soup (special) and pancake tonight. I go on watch and let Christopher enjoy it hot. Suddenly all hell is let loose. The port boom rises in the air and the spinnaker disappears in the night. It is retrieved. The cringle has gone. Sleep is uneasy as all our ears are waiting.

3

21*st day*. A ragged day with water slopping over the decks. We find uncooked pudding (crumble) not unpleasant.

22*nd day*. The spotlight is knocked over and won't work. Great seas are rolling along but the wind is light. A wisp of smoke or a steamer's bridge would be a welcome sight. My sole contribution to life today was to wash the tea-towel.

23*rd day*. The world is fresh; dark blue seas marching and a happy rushing sound. The newly-made cake is all right until Peter stands on it. He has a cupful of crumbs and we finish the ginger cake. An odd uneven sea, and one stood on end and poured itself down the open fo'c'sle hatch. Cries of rage below.

24*th day*. Peter's birthday. It takes an hour to change into fore and aft rig so that I can mend the spinnaker. After chicken, asparagus, chocolate mousse and Martinique wine we leave Peter with Venus and the moon.

25*th day*. I invent a switch for the binnacle with a cork, two aerial wires and a match. It works. The afternoon sun is before the mast and throws shadows on the rigging. The cabin is quiet but a different set of dishes is rattling.

26*th day*. Rain, and I am dreaming of hot soup when cold biscuits are thrust through the hatch. Into the peace of the afternoon, a cry . . . the boom and sail flail and our port spinnaker is gone. The waves to port are dashed flat and the tops blown. P. and C. retrieve the ruins and I go below to make scones. Weevils in the rice.

27*th day*. Wet and squally and Christopher glancing often behind him after yesterday's catastrophe. I examine the ravished spinnaker and with Peter's help cut a strip of new canvas 3½ inches wide and 125 inches long. Reefed the main after dinner.

28*th day*. Sewing spinnaker. The others take my watches and make drop scones for tea.

29*th day*. Christopher reports the loss of the log spinner, the last. No one says very much.

30*th day*. While I am sitting on the foredeck mending the spinnaker Peter comes up to make a strop. He half lowers the sail in my face and it takes off my hat. I protest. It flops off my only pair of glasses into the sea. Peter is so sorry that he drops my last marline spike overboard. I am very full of rage and quite sad.

31*st day*. The gaff jaws give where they were welded in Camarinas. We sail under trysail and one spinnaker and later add the genoa. Peter chisels at the gaff all day to make it fit an old boom fitting. Christopher, helping him, talks about drinking port at Barreiro and makes P. cross. The work is heavy but he fits the metal on and screws it in. C. files off the nut holding the bolt. Not having caught a fish since leaving England we had to catch one today. It was a shark. We haul it alongside and lasso its tail and Christopher shoots it. It tastes like cotton wool.

32nd day. The fitting doesn't work. Experiments with reversed bolts and filed pins. Christopher pours water over himself and his mouth is too dry to eat.

33rd day. As the sky lightens we turned out. I left my bunk ready for my promised return but it stayed till night. The sail was hoisted; Peter, aloft, watched it. Trouble. . . . Brass screws were replaced by old steel ones. Supports are filed to fit. I clean the galley and paint-work, take the helm for trial and error of sail setting, carry up grape juice and a late lunch. By evening we are under one reefed main, top-sail and spinnaker. Peter is queer and trembly and I fall into a drugged sleep. Waking is unpleasant but my night watch is cool and tranquil. An empty tin glittered for an hour in our wake.

34th day. The spinnaker is now sewn and ready for an emergency set-ting. Thunder and lightning in the night.

35th day. Peter comes up in the night, the light gone from his eyes. "A coral patch," he mutters; then he wakes and goes back to bed.

36th day. The breeze is unhappy, trying to pry under the sail and toss-ing the topsail like a blown leaf. My patch in the old spinnaker is giving where the forestay rubs. Peter is reading *The Chinese Room* but he puts the cringle in the head of my spinnaker and sets it. I mend the other. My eyes are fuzzy with sewing, the dim compass and the sea.

37th day. The moon röse behind a bank of floating figures. All the clouds today turn to islands, but it is Christopher who sees Fatu Hiva first and we turn towards it, not sure which it is until P.'s noon sight tells us the way to Hiva Oa. I wash my hair and itch less. Christopher shaves and smells of scented soap.

38th day. I wake to the sound of Christopher's voice offering me por-ridge and go up on deck. The whole beauty of the island bursts upon me in glistening green; coconut palms on the shore, steep, furrowed slopes rising to the peak of a great mountain in a wispy nest of cloud. Waves pound on the rocks, white streaks turn into waterfalls, Hanake Island stands like a silhouette in the sunlight, the white and red of the little light structure peeps through the trees and out of the bay comes a schooner with men, bananas and copra. A man in a white helmet raises his hand in greeting.

Under Black Point and into Taa Huku bay we sailed with

a dying breeze. A horseman, bronzed, with his hand shading his eyes, gazed down upon us. With a great shout, "Teei-oo" ringing round the steep walls of this narrow place he turned his horse and galloped down the path towards the village.

As the mainsail was lowered our Heath Robinson gaff collapsed and it was with some surprise that we turned to a greeting at our side, A tall blond young man gripped our rail.

"My name," he said, "is Lamberty."

CHAPTER FIVE

A MARQUESAN HOLIDAY

INTO the very bay where we now were anchored Lamberty had sailed his converted lifeboat *Kroja* from Holland three years before. He had walked up the shady path, over Black Point and down into Atuona and there he had met Rebecca the chief's daughter. All sense of time and of the safety of the ship seemed to desert him until late that evening a horseman galloped down the road with the news that *Kroja* had dragged on to the beach and was now being pounded by the waves. The whole village turned out to try and save her but it was too late. *Kroja* was a total loss. Lamberty stayed on.

One day a Belgian yacht bound for Hawaii came into Taa Huku bay. Seeing a chance of returning to Holland to find another boat Lamberty rowed out and offered himself as crew.

"Wait for me, Rebecca, for one year," he told her, and sailed.

They put into Caroline Island for water, found none, ran the ship on a coral head, and pumping her watch and watch, sailed on to Christmas Island, six hundred miles away.

Back in Holland, Lamberty found a publisher for the book he had been writing, became master of the *Anna Elizabeth* and set sail to keep his tryst with Rebecca. His long forced passage with an untried crew may well have been the reason for the events in Post Office Bay.

When I first saw Rebecca she was like an untamed gazelle, wary and still but when she smiled it was as sun chasing shadow. They made a handsome pair but a man whose ambition it was to sail round the world non-stop, might, we thought, be a difficult person to follow for a girl with only one sound lung, and almost prostrate with seasickness. They were planning to sail back to Holland, but we wondered what would happen if they got so far and Rebecca could go no farther. I could see that Rebecca, from the way she looked at him, wondered that too.

R. L. Stevenson once said that the view from Black Point

was the finest in the world. The sweep of the bay, the Pacific rollers thundering on the curving beach a hundred feet below, the sultry valley, the red roofs peeping through the palm trees, the heavy scented air of an island sleeping off the excesses of its turbulent past; an island now inhabited by a dispirited and listless people, we had been told, forlorn remnant of its savage healthy tribes. But the French have a cure for this which is saving the Marquesans from the Carib's fate. Mixed blood is producing a stronger race and for the first time the population is on the increase.

At the hospital, small framed buildings in the same compound as the doctor's bungalow and shaded by trees and bougainvillea, Dr Stern never knew when he did his round what patients he was likely to see. Some might have gone home for the day, or have changed places with others who needed a rest. "They are half wild," he said, "and if you were to treat them like Europeans they'd die. We try and make them so happy they'll want to come back." He had been most impressed by the results of streptomycin and thought that the battle against tubercle had been almost won.

Once every six weeks, sometimes twice, the island schooner *Vaitere* (Running Water) sails into the bay. There is mail, a new face or two; there are stores, pigs and wine; and that night no light will shine from Black Point, for there will be no one capable of walking up the path to put a match to it. A benevolent government, which rations wine to the Marquesans at two litres a month, says nothing about not drinking it in one night.

For three weeks we sailed among the islands. *La poste* (three letters) had to be delivered to Ua Pu and the doctor's family were badly in need of vegetables that only grew at Nukuhiva. A three-quarter-inch bolt and stronger plates from poor *Kroja's* remains now held our gaff aloft and we sailed for Hanamanu on the north coast. We arrived at night; a huge buttress of rock dividing the bay in two and standing like a medieval fortress against the sky was our only guide.

If ever I were to be shipwrecked I would pray that it might be at Hanamanu. I could live on bananas big and small, yellow and pink, on coconuts and lemons, breadfruit and taro, all in great profusion and growing wild. There is a trail, now overgrown but still possible to follow, lined by purple flowers and orange blooms like orchids that leads towards the mountains and a great plateau where game runs wild.

In a clearing behind the foreshore lived a handful of copra pickers. When we asked for some drinking nuts they mistook our meaning and offered us spirit distilled from the flower of coconuts. It had a kick that made absinthe seem like water. We had stumbled on an illicit still.

The village of Hakahetau on the island of Ua Pu is some sixty miles to the north-west and has the reputation of being hard to find. The only chart I had was a drawing of its salient features and a lifelike picture of a cave, by the doctor, on the back of an envelope. This cave, he said, was important because by the time you saw it you had passed the village. I saw the cave all right, and then looked back through the glasses and found the village tucked right into the head of a bay within a bay, dwarfed behind by pinnacles of rock which would have made a perfect setting for a story by Poe and illustrated by Rackham.

We dropped anchor on the place marked on the envelope, watched the seas tumbling on the pebble beach and swirling over the peninsula of rock where the doctor had told us to land. Soon a pirogue, manned by a tall Marquesan (the bluer the blood the taller the man) came out to welcome us with bananas and a couple of fish caught that morning. Haki then explained, in excellent French, what we ourselves could see, that it would be wiser if he took us ashore and so avoided *l'ecrasement du canot*. Choosing the largest wave to sweep him up that stony shore he landed us with great skill and directed us to the Valots' house.

Under scattered palm trees, past native huts roofed with pandanus leaves, with coconut matting on the earthen floor for beds, and both ends open to the winds of heaven, at the head of a procession of children, women and men, we ended up at the schoolhouse where the Valots stood to welcome us.

Claude Valot was a pale young man with limpid eyes who had been a chartered accountant, an instructor of parachute

troops, a *Directeur de banque de l'Indo-Chine à Tahiti* before re-
nouncing the world, as he put it, to come and teach the French
language to the inhabitants of this island, who had had to
manage up to now without this inestimable benefit. His house,
built of wood and not unlike a suburban bungalow, was neat
and trim and very hot, and he and his charming wife showed us
over this and the school with as much enthusiasm as their
singular detachment allowed.

That night we dined with them. Quantities of raw fish
soaked in *citron* and served with coconut cream were followed
by sucking-pig, with a hibiscus flower in its ear, roasted whole
with baked breadfruit, sweet potatoes, poi and a bottle of
Burgundy. The great meal, the wine, the scented night,
Claude's slow didactic speech, produced in me a philosophic
mood, and I thought what an introvert one would have to be
to live contentedly alone with one's wife and with only books
and a gramophone as contact with what we call civilization.
To have lived within the boundaries of a great city, to have
seen the world at war at your very doorstep, to have made
close friends; these things, I thought would prevent me from
ever wanting to live in a South Sea island where the talk of
fish and coconuts and the daily village life would be the only
stimulus to existence. I was full of admiration for the Valots,
but I could not envy them.

After dinner Haki came to tell us there was a swell rolling
in and that we must not delay. Our host took his paraffin
lamp to light the scene, and we walked down to the landing,
where a small crowd, not wishing to miss the fun, had collected. Haki got his outrigger away and then paddled round
to the rocky peninsula upon which we were standing. Riding a
long sea, using his paddle as helm and backing water at the
same time, Haki brought his outrigger in, level with our feet.
"Jump," he shouted to Anne who did so and the next moment
the canoe was five feet down. Christopher and I followed
each in turn.

The next day Haki made us a present of a *tiki*. It was of
flint and had a long, sharp leading edge. Valot told us that it
was a tool used by the natives in the time of Captain Cook. He

also told us that Haki had once swum six miles out to sea in rough weather to rescue a man from a sailing canoe. Before we sailed we gave him wire trace, hooks and a lure, and he in turn tried to tell us how to catch fish, but that, we thought, was beyond even the powers of Haki.

A fresh trade wind bore us swiftly over the twenty miles of sea between Ua Pu and Nuku Hiva, and it was noon when we made in between the Sentinels lying guard at each side of Tai O Hae just over a hundred years after Herman Melville so entered in the whaler *Dolly*, and here is how he describes (in *Typee*) the welcome accorded to that tired ship:

We were still some distance from the beach and under slow headway, when we sailed into the midst of these swimming nymphs, and they boarded us at every quarter; many seizing hold of the chain plates and springing into the chains; others, at the peril of being run over by the vessel in her course, catching at the bob-stays, and wreathing their slender forms about the ropes, hung suspended in the air. All of them at length succeeded in getting up the ship's sides, where they clung dripping with the brine, and glowing from the bath, their jet black tresses streaming over their shoulders, and half enveloping their otherwise naked forms. There they hung, sparkling with savage vivacity, laughing gaily at one another, and chattering away with infinite glee. Nor were they idle the while, for each performed the simple offices of the toilet for the other. Their luxuriant locks, wound up and twisted into the smallest possible compass, were freed from the briny element; the whole person carefully dried and from a little round shell that passed from hand to hand, anointed with a fragrant oil; their adornments were completed by passing a few loose folds of white tappa, in a modest cincture, around the waist. Thus arrayed, they no longer hesitated but flung themselves lightly over the bulwarks, and were quickly frollicking about the decks. Many of them went forward, perching upon the head-rails, or running out upon the bowsprit, while others seated themselves upon the taffrail, or reclined at full length upon the boats. What a sight for us sailors!

How avoid so dire a temptation? For who could think of tumbling these artless creatures overboard, when they had swum miles to welcome us?

Where were these maidens now? The port was deserted and a group of Marquesans stood forlornly upon the beach. Black clouds lay heavily on the mountain peaks and there was a feeling of gloom that was in keeping with the rain that now fell in torrents.

Arming ourselves with "insect repellent" against the ravages of the nau-nau fly, so different from the "fragrant oils" of Melville's maidens, we went ashore to find Bob McKitterick, the trader, playing patience with his Marquesan wife. For forty years Bob, from Yorkshire, had lived among these islands. He was getting old. We chatted over a bottle of beer and a plate of mangoes of all the people whom we had read about and he had known; Muhlhauser and Robinson, Temple Utley who had been at St. George's Hospital when I was there and Commander Graham and his daughter Margaret and, more recently, the Crowes, the Hiscocks, and the Greggs of *Novia* who had sailed less than a week ago. Just before that, said Bob, a ketch flying the Swedish flag, had worked her way into the bay and then, to his amazement, had worn ship and sailed out again. Since the time they were nearly cast upon the breakwater at La Palma and Sten had discovered that he couldn't tow her with the outboard, the Homdahls had taken a wary view of landlocked anchorages with feckless puffs of wind inside them.

As soon as we had read our mail, cashed a cheque with Bob, given him some copper nails for his sloop, walked up a brown and yellow stream to look at the bay from above, filled our water-tanks, bought a few tins (at forty per cent over their price at Tahiti for freightage), we said good-bye to him and his family and left him staring out to sea. Bob had a growing conviction, he told us, that soon, in a week or a month, his son, whom he had not heard of for fifteen years would be sailing into this bay.

But if Nuku Hiva had been rather disappointing we were to see a glimpse of the old Marquesas reflected in the new.

Following the *Anna Elizabeth* we sailed into Hanehavane on the island of Tahu Ata; a difficult bit of pilotage without an engine, involving two right-angle bends, a passage forty feet wide and two hundred yards long between two underwater banks of coral and the entrance to the lagoon itself marked by two stakes twenty feet apart with a rock in the middle, over which there might, we hoped, be six feet of water. Inside the lagoon as if to welcome us to the gates of heaven, or to bury us if we failed to make it, stood a priest in a long canoe manned by many dusky paddlers.

We had come for a scrub, for this is the only place, we had been told, where there was a rise and fall of five feet. We put an anchor out astern, ran the ship ashore on the sandy beach and tied her up to a palm tree. *Ffavoa*, the doctor's boat, came tearing in, swaying from side to side as her crew of Marquesan girls crowded the rails first on one side and then the other. The tide receded, each mast took on its own peculiar angle, the girls, their bright pareus streaming away from their bodies, swam, like schools of dolphin, from ship to ship till the copper shone like warming pans. They swarmed aboard sitting, on the bulwarks like Melville's nymphs "sparkling with savage vivacity and chattering with infinite glee".

The sun went down, a fire was lit, the circle grew as each ship's company joined it. The crackling flames, the murmur of voices, a note of song, the dim shape of Hiva Oa across the moonlit water, suddenly made me wonder if life in the South Sea islands would in fact be as insupportable as I had thought.

CHAPTER SIX

A CLOUD OF ISLANDS

BETWEEN the Marquesas and the Societies lie the Atolls, known to the early Polynesians as the Paumotus, or "Cloud of Islands". To navigators they have another name, the low archipelago, for few of them (none in the north-west sector) are more than a few feet above the water. Some are circles of coral with lagoons inside looking on the chart like wedding-rings, some have lyrical names like Mangareva and one of them, Anaa, whose lagoon is shallow, reflects an image of itself into the sky in a beautiful pale green colour to be seen from a great distance. But in thick weather, the currents unpredictable, the Trade Wind blowing at half a gale, they earn other names, the Isles of Disappointment and the Dangerous Archipelago.

For these islands we set sail, the wind being fair and light. On the first night when I went up to relieve Christopher for his dinner I noticed that the gaff jaws had capsized and were tearing at the copper sheathing round the mast. "Good God!" I cried. "How long has that been going on?"

"Not long, Peter. I noticed it after you'd gone below but I didn't want to disturb your dinner."

Our new bolt was badly bent. Using the Primus as a forge I made half a dozen not altogether successful attempts to straighten it in the vice, then took the helm and gave Christopher the job of setting all sail. He came aft looking as our Benjamin used to after chasing a chicken. "I'm terribly sorry," he said. "I think you'd better try and get someone else at Tahiti."

"Go on down and get your dinner," I growled.

I lit my pipe and my sharpened senses relaxed. The moon flooded the ship with a strong, clear light.

"Thought you said we were a university," groaned the gaff jaws. "Your job is to teach . . . to *teach* . . ." squeaked the blocks.

I called Christopher.

"If I haven't made a seaman of you by the time we get to British Columbia, you'd better go home. It'll be my fault," I said.

Five days out from Tahuata I took my sight at noon and, on working out my position, found we were only seven miles from Takaroa. There had been nothing to be seen from the deck. Anne clambered up the ratlines.

"Come and see," she called. "It looks like grass growing out of a blue lawn."

All that afternoon we half drifted, half sailed down the western shore of the atoll. It was made up of small islets, some grey, some pink, and in between were gaps where green water lay in pools on the reef. Through these gaps the eye caught glimpses of a lagoon so wide that the distant shore could not be seen. By nightfall we were still a few miles off the pass into the lagoon. Banks of cloud piled high above the island, rain came down in torrents and the wind boxed the compass. It was most difficult to judge our position for one lot of trees looked exactly like another. Anne kept the ship off and on, while Christopher and I, fearing we should want to use the engine to get through the pass, bent double beside its silent body trying, by unsticking both exhaust valves, making a new carbon brush out of Anne's drawing pencil, clearing the jet and doing half a dozen other things whose nature I have now forgotten, to coax it into life.

I straightened my back and looked out to find the moon was up, the sea calm and Anne asleep against the bulwarks. Feeling aggrieved I nearly woke her up, but on second thoughts Christopher and I turned in, the less anxious for knowing that if there was any danger she would immediately wake up.

At dawn Anne was taking out the kinks induced by cramp. On shore a black, forlorn shape resolved itself into the wreck of the *County of Roxburgh*, once a four-masted barque, lying high and dry on the coral sand. Christopher swung the heavy fly-wheel, the engine burst into life and we motored down the coast until huts, bungalows and a tiny church revealed the village, and the swirling outcoming tide, the pass. By keeping within a few feet of a coral bank we edged in inch by inch to come alongside the stone quay within a few feet of *Novia*.

When two voyagers meet again everything must wait until the insatiable curiosity of each for the other's adventures (and the pleasure of recounting his own) is satisfied. With a single mind we leapt aboard *Novia* to sit in her capacious cabin and without pausing for breath we each recounted our adventures. *Novia* had left Panama two hours before we did, had anchored at Gardner Bay twelve hours before we got there and slipped out at dawn, had visited the Wittmers' the day we left and had made a fast passage to Ua Huka in the Marquesas in twenty-seven days before a fine steady Trade; which shows how very different two voyages across the same bit of ocean at the same time of the year can be. This encounter was providential, because Lee had a bronze bolt with which we replaced our bent one, and not until that was done did we step ashore.

The village was almost deserted, only an old, old woman with eyes aglow and a spring in her walk as if she might break into a hula gave us the native greeting, "*Ia ora na*", and a thin black dog which walked slowly out into the lagoon to search on the drying reefs for fish. If times were hard, Lee said, the natives eat the dogs. At slack water he and Christopher went swimming, Lee scanning the depths through his underwater goggles. Suddenly he scrambled out on to the reef.

"Chris!" he shouted. "There's three sharks down there. Let's go scare them away."

Without waiting for a reply, he dived. Christopher, after a fraction of a second, followed him. Knowing how he dreaded these brutes, I thought he must have felt a little like Sir Arthur Grimble when he was offered, with truly Polynesian hospitality, the opportunity to become human bait for octopus.

In the evening a canoe came over from the pearl diving village. Lines were baited and flung into the pass as the flood came in, and within a few minutes a shark was hauled triumphantly ashore. Seven feet of snapping, fighting fish, thrashing in the dust while Tiariki, long-handled knife in hand, waited like a matador for the kill. In a flash he was on to the shark's back, the knife plunged in below the head and out of reach again almost before our eyes had registered the attack.

Tiariki, like most of the young Tahitians, spoke fluent French, and he offered to pilot us in to the lagoon, an offer we gladly accepted for we had been warned by the *Pacific Island Pilot*, Vol. III, that "the eastern end of the pass is barred by a coral reef except for a small channel through its northern end, with a rectangular bend in it, which gives access to the lagoon; the currents in this channel are very strong, local knowledge is essential and it should be used only in the case of necessity."

Under Tiariki's eye *Moonraker* swept safely through at slack water, her decks crowded with men and girls, and towing three pirogues. Distant trees grew larger as we ploughed our way over the mirrored lake, huts appeared, and a procession of young girls dressed in white (for it was Sunday) walked into the Mormon Church from which came the lively, rhythmic singing of Tahitian songs. Tiariki grinned.

"They sing in church," he said, "but they sing of love."

Scarcely had our passengers gone when the gendarme came out.

"Where is your permit to land on this island?" he asked; and when I told him that I had none because I was told that none was necessary, he said, "You are the third yacht in three years to come here without a permit. You must leave at once."

I asked him aboard, gave him a glass of Dubonnet, a little cognac and a large dose of my most persuasive French. We could stay, he told us, till morning.

That night he came again. He said, "I understand you are a doctor of medicine, Monsieur?"

"That is so."

"My little boy has a fever and is sick. Would Monsieur come and see him?"

The gendarme's hut was at the end of what might be called the village street. The glare from an Aladdin lamp fell on the plaited walls of coconut fronds, the roof of pandanus leaves and on the pale, worried face of his young wife who had only just come out from Paris to "this savage island". The child was sick, but I was more relieved than I care to admit when I found that I was not faced with an acute appendix. In a day or two, I reassured the mother, her boy would be well again.

By the time I got back to the shore a wind had sprung up. The trees swayed like ships under sail, and now and then a coconut fell with a thud upon the ground. I walked to the windward side and watched the seas marching against the island like Roman cohorts. My face was whipped by spray. It was nothing more than a strong breeze, but I remembered the wreck of the sailing ship on the reef outside. Hurricanes are not common in this part of the Pacific, but it would be a little like living in a great industrial city in the Atomic Age. One would never quite know.

My patient improved and, as you can imagine, I heard no more about permits, but news in such a village does not take long to travel, and when the natives found that he had indeed recovered, they suddenly remembered they had seen no doctor for at least three years and all their half-forgotten pains came back to them with redoubled vigour. A practice was born overnight.

Lee has described this place as a boom village, a sort of Tuamotuan counterpart of the Californian gold rush, for men came here from Manihi and Ahe, from Arutua and Rangiroa for the pearl diving. A good diver might well earn fifteen hundred dollars in a season. A bicycle, an outboard motor for his pirogue, a coloured American shirt and tins of bully beef from Australia bought from the Chinese storekeeper where he banks his pearl shell, are the measure of his wealth. At the end of the season he sells all and has one glorious fling at Carnival time at Tahiti, and two months later works his passage back to his own island, broke.

The day we rowed out to watch the pearl diving, sound carried over the water like an echo in a valley. The cries of the divers extending their lungs before *la plongée*, a yodelling sound and a curious whistling shriek, mingled with the chatter of the boat crews across the placid water. We found Tiariki with his head just above the water, his goggles on and about to dive. A boy of fifteen stood in the stern with a coil of light line at his feet attached to a twenty-five-pound weight which

Sparkling with savage vivacity

One brown leg on the tiller and his voice in full song

Tiariki held in his hand while making the descent. Another, thicker rope led down into the depths and was attached to the basket into which Tiariki put the shells a hundred and twenty feet below. Through a wooden box with a glass bottom I watched him go. It was like a slow-motion film, smooth and effortless and from the time he started to the time he came back was a few seconds under three minutes.

In Polynesia it is easier to arrive than to depart. At the time we were due to leave canoes put out from the shore, headed by the Chief, who put aboard a sack of oranges and his hat band that Anne had admired for the lovely colouring of the tiny shells from which it was made. An old man whose grandson I had treated for fluid on the lung and arranged (I hope) for transfer to hospital at Tahiti, gave me a basketful of the most delicate cowrie shells. Girls with flowers behind their ears put *leis* round our necks and it was with the greatest difficulty that I persuaded our pilot to start. I knew that the tide would already be racing out through the channel into the pass. Our pilot was very old, could speak no French and, I discovered soon after leaving the village, was almost blind.

We were three-quarters of the way across the lagoon when we overtook a couple in a pirogue. In answer to our pilot's shout the girl jumped aboard. She turned to me, "*Monsieur, le vieux demande que la machine va beaucoup plus vite.*" I went up the ratlines. The current, I could see, was sweeping through the channel at a good ten knots, the water, as black and smooth as tar, poured round the bend, while an eddy, pale green over sand, ran in the reverse direction.

The reef, drying out in places, was at the turn knife-edged, but as long as the ship could be controlled by her helm she should be able to negotiate that turn. Christopher and Anne were standing by the mast, silent.

"We'll try it," I said.

Moonraker gathered way with incredible velocity, heading straight for the reef. Our pilot struggled to put the helm up for the bend, but *Moonie* had the bit between her teeth and to this day Anne swears that our bowsprit overhung that coral. I sprang at the tiller, the old man's belly between it and the

4

bulwarks, squeezing until he grunted for breath. The ship came round. Our pilot's face was running with sweat, not all of which, I thought, was due to exertion. Thank God for a night at sea!

I don't quite know how we ever got into Ahé; the sun was already in the west when I saw that violent tide boiling out of the twenty-five-yard-wide pass, forcing its way far out to sea. But there was a fine beam wind, we set the genoa, the ship heeled far over, and inch by inch we overcame it until we got to the trees where the wind was cut off. We started the engine and were still taken back, we sailed first to one side and then to the other, but that tide had us beaten. And then, without warning, the wind switched, and for about ten minutes blew hard into the pass, and by the time it changed we were through the worst and sailing into the lagoon. But this had taken time and the sun was getting low, nor was there a ghost of a sign of a village. That there was a village at all was only by word of mouth; none was marked on the chart.

Suddenly to the north-west a column of smoke rose into the air. Piloted by two young men each with a flower behind his right ear we came to an anchorage behind a reef. The village gathered on the beach. They led us to a long bench on which we sat drinking green drinking-nuts, the women plaited poinsettias and a white flower like the Tiara Tahiti into leis, they took us by the hand to their fishing pool where bright green parrot-fish swam over the pink coral bottom and to the water hole through which clear water welled. It tasted only slightly brackish.

That night as we sat at dinner we became aware that our ship was full of people. Brown faces looked down upon us, through the hatch and the skylights, and a girl's voice whispered, "*Anne, Anne, du vin, s'il vous plait!*" Tiahe seized our Madeira *machete*, an instrument with five strings, found two of them broken and sent Horu, his wife, for catgut. As the moon rose over the trees our company started to sing. The rhythm is as bold and accurate as that of a Calypso, but it has a haunting quality that the Calypso lacks. Tiahe, who had had more than one glass of wine, suddenly burst into a savage tune, summoning Horu to dance. Slim, very dark, her mouth turned down at the corners, Horu rose; her face was a mask, her movements sensual, provoking and utterly primitive. Cassimi, Head Man, joined her. Faster and faster grew the tempo of the music, the more savage the movements within the tiny compass of the bridge-deck while the onlookers stamped their feet in unison. And then, as tension mounted to a peak, Tiahe stopped and the dancers sank to the deck.

Four days later they accompanied us to the pass, a large pirogue towing behind; Tiahe, a ruff of poinsettias round his neck, a flower behind his ear, one brown foot on the tiller, his voice in full song, while Cassimi stood by the mast, a bronze statue in a straw hat. He pointed up at our spread of canvas, swelling before the breeze.

"Too much sail," he cried, "so soon will you be gone."

The pass was upon us. We watched them set their sail and wave and wave and finally turn away. I watched Horu stow her trophy in the bottom of the boat. She had carried away my favourite hat.

CHAPTER SEVEN

TAHITI

OUR course through the main chain of atolls lay between Rangiroa and Arutua. Towards this gap, no more than a gate in a hedge of atolls, we ran before a fresh south-easterly breeze. The night was dark and overcast, and with no observations to check the uncertainty of the currents I stood on the upper ratlines trying vainly to enlarge my horizon.

Anne's shout came from the deck, "Copra! Can you smell it?"

I could indeed, and over the port quarter was a thin line of trees and the white of broken water. Ahead the gate lay open and with the lightness of spirit that every navigator feels when the most recent danger lies astern, I worked out a course for Venus Point on Tahiti.

Papeete, the capital of Tahiti, has been called the Paris of the South Seas. The uneven houses along the waterfront, the honking of horns, the ringing of bicycle bells, the smell of garlic. And when it rained, and the water rattled down on the iron roofs of the Chinese restaurants and ran down the yellow gutters, and bent old women stood in doorways, and canned music blared out from lighted windows, it was so like a scene from a Rene Clair film that I half expected Jean Gabin to come strolling down the pavement.

The Americans had their own idea of what life should be like in the South Seas; barbecues on the beach, a vahine or two and all the modern conveniences of the U.S.A. In the background is the island itself, for which Papeete is but a mask. Valleys and mountains as yet unexplored, great peaks each inhabited by its own familiar spirit and unclimbable by man, a lake which legend has it is inhabited by eels with ears; where natives live very much as they did two hundred years ago, and where strange things still happen. There was the Tahitian schoolmaster who went to teach on a Tuamotuan atoll, fell in love with an island girl and had two sons. When the time came for him to return he told his vahine that he must leave her but that the two boys must go with him to Papeete to be taught. Prostrate with grief she swore that she would lay a curse on the children if he left without her, but, deaf to all her entreaties, he sailed. Some months later the elder boy fell sick, was taken to hospital, grew rapidly worse and within a week was dead. No medical evidence for his illness could be found. Then the second boy fell sick, but again the doctors could give no diagnosis or offer any hope. In desperation the schoolmaster took the dying boy in his arms and walked to a far valley where there lived an old woman of whom he had heard in his childhood as an exorciser of evil spirits. He came to her hut at night and implored her help. The old woman laid the boy on a bed of leaves and touched his eyes.

"You are in time," she said, "come for him in seven days. He will be well."

Our lives, for the short time we were there, were closely bound up with the waterfront, our friends among the New Zealand and American yachtsmen, but even here the spell of the island was disturbing, and I remember at a party one night after Ross Norgrove had been singing Maori songs on *White Squall*, he suddenly turned and said, "You don't want to go to British Columbia among all that snow and ice. Come to New Zealand with us." And almost before we knew what we were saying our plans had been changed.

Then in the morning some incident, so small that I have completely forgotten it, changed them back again. Anne was on deck at the time and what I call the "Look" came into her face. I have only seen it twice, but I know better than to challenge it. She said that to change our whole voyage at this stage was ridiculous, that she was doubtful if we could finish the voyage in less than three years, and that this would be adding a fourth, and that it was too long to be "scattered about the world in a boat" and that the crew you knew was better than the crew you didn't and that she for one had no wish "to change horses in midstream". What had threatened to become a tense situation ended in a roar of laughter at this agile mixing of metaphor and rather to our relief our brief madness was over.

One morning I was walking along the quay with the head customs officer. He pointed to a small boat tied to an enormous buoy in the middle of the harbour. She looked a mere toy.

He said, "D'you know where she's come from?"

I shook my head.

"Her last port was Valparaiso and she has come round the Horn from east to west in winter."

M. Bardieu had been a punt-builder on the Seine and had taken seven years to build his sloop (she was nineteen feet on the waterline). He made her as indestructible as it was possible to do with so small a vessel. He could steer from inside the cabin, and there was an almost waterproof cover over most of the cockpit to protect him from the weather.

Marcel Bardieu was a stocky little Frenchman who had a charmingly naïve way of minimizing the obvious dangers of such a voyage. He had had, he said, no intention of rounding the Horn in winter, but he was knocked overboard by the boom when some six hundred miles north of this region and had to spend many weeks in hospital. By the time he came out the summer was over, so what could he do but go on? As he was beating down Lemaire Strait between Staten Island and Tierra del Fuego a gale blew up which, with a nine-knot tide running against it, caused a "confused" sea. His vessel capsized twice in the same morning, and a fifty-pound anchor lashed to the cabin floor broke adrift. (I have seen the mark on the cabin roof) and damaged both the vessel and himself. He carried on, but after rounding Cape Horn the weather became so bad that he ran for one of the fiords where a small vessel can take shelter. Ross was with us at the time and I remember his rugged face suddenly wrinkling into a great grin, "Doc!" he cried, "I guess this guy is made of something different to you and me!" I guess Ross is right.

Among the many fine vessels in Papeete harbour was William Albert Robinson's brigantine. I cherished a very faint hope that we might meet him and we nearly did. A friend of ours had driven us round the island, and on the way home we saw a tall white-haired figure with stooping shoulders and rather protruding lips. Our friend was about to apply his brakes when he changed his mind. "That's Robinson of *Svaap*," he said, "but I can see from his back (Robinson was earnestly contemplating a ditch) that this is not one of his days for being interested in other people."

Complete with our new gaff fitting, loaded down with two months' stores, we sailed from Tahiti on a Monday. The scent of Tiara Tahiti was born on the off-shore breeze as we sailed slowly towards the pass. We threw overboard our leis. And then, suddenly, the wind changed, blowing briskly from the sea, so perhaps our leis did drift back to the shore and will compel us, in the tradition of the island, to return before we die.

CHAPTER EIGHT

LES ÎLES SOUS LE VENT

FROM its appearance on the chart Moorea is shaped like a heart with its apex facing south. It is, like Tahiti, entirely surrounded by a reef, and between this and the shore are deep lagoons and narrow channels, scattered coral heads and shallows. On the northern side, along which we were now sailing, two passes, only to be identified by the absence of broken water, led into two deep indentations which seemed to penetrate to the very heart of the mountains, whose splintered outlines give to the island its look of fantasy. We chose the second of these, and as we beat in a little wind came rustling down the valley.

During the night I woke with a start. I went up on deck. The bay was filled with stippled light from the moon that hung suspended from a cloudless sky, and silvery shadows danced upon the water.

The stillness was absolute.

There was something very queer about that valley—as if the outraged gods were contemplating violence on this unwelcome intruder; nor would my heightened senses have been surprised to hear the beat of drums or to see a long canoe pulling out from the darkened shore. Gradually the sense of danger lessened and I cast about for some explanation of my curious state. It might, of course, have been the moon but I am not usually moon-struck, I am not psychic, nor do I usually imagine things that do not exist. All I know was that I felt like a dog whose hairs bristled with apprehension. Then it passed and I have never felt it again.

Along the sandy path to the village those passers-by that we met seemed strangely silent after the people of Tahiti. We had the same impression of the village, a straggling place, until we came to a store owned by a Tahitian woman married to a Chinese. Her laughing toothless face seemed to infect all her customers. She found mangoes and the island pamplemousse—

a fruit half orange, half grapefruit, and better than either—and she hustled a small boy into shinning up a coconut tree for nuts; she even hinted at eggs. She took our air mail letters to give to the captain of the island boat who would post them at Tahiti. The money? "Oh, leave that till next week," she cried, "the captain will tell me how much."

We became known as "*le petit bateau anglais d'Urofara*". Our bread and stores arrived by mule ridden by the boy-friend of the girl in the hut behind the cove; a girl whose face and form seemed made for a painting by Gauguin. But when I went for fish I had to go early. It would still be dark, and the sound of the conch shells echoed round the hills as each little canoe with its flare in the stern like a glow-worm, crept up the bay. At the village shadowy figures came stealing out of the huts, and in a few minutes all the catch would be sold and the canoes hauled up on the beach.

Farther up the bay lived Mr Kellum the planter whose house, built on stilts, overlooked Robinson Cove. It was at his suggestion that we went round to Paopao to see MacDonald the painter. "He's been here for nearly forty years and knows more about the islands than anyone."

We paid several visits to Mr MacDonald's hut, right on the water's edge but never found him in till the night before we left, when we went at dusk. The door was open, but no sound came from the darkened room.

"Is anyone in?" called Anne.

"Who's that?" came a voice.

"A fellow Scot to see you."

"You'd better come in, all the same."

Our host lit a candle, stuck it in the mouth of a bottle and glared at us with the aid of its light.

"Aren't you off the yacht? Is one of you a doctor? I loathe yachtsmen and hate doctors. I hear the government has put you in your place and you'll soon be let in by the back door; where you belong."

Nettled by this sudden attack on a profession I have no reason to despise (and wondering if it had anything to do with an ulcer half hidden behind a pad of cotton wool),

I said "You seem to share the views of Mr Bernard Shaw."

"Shaw? Yes, I knew Shaw well; we were contemporaries. He wrote a few good plays but he never had any ideas. He borrowed those from James Joyce."

The room was full of shadows. Our host sat on an upturned packing case while Christopher leaned against the wall, and Anne and I sat on the only two chairs. He opened a bottle of wine.

Whatever he thought of doctors (or yachtsmen) Mac-Donald loved the Tahitians.

"Damn fools, the French," he exclaimed, "they call 'em lazy but they're nothing of the sort. They've found the right way to live and they've the guts not to be stampeded out of it. I've seen 'em after a hurricane's wiped out all they've got. They'll work like niggers and laugh while they're doing it. Children? They're the most adult people in the world."

He strode round the tiny room.

"You must go now. I go to bed when the sun sets, and it's long past that now."

He shepherded us towards the door, and as we walked away from that lonely place his harsh voice followed us into the night, "Come and see me again."

The passage on which we now embarked was rather less than a hundred miles. The wind was fair, and during the night (under the light of a waning moon) I sighted the mountains of Huahine fine on the starboard bow. The aura of mystery with which I endowed it took my mind back to a book by Peter Buck about the migration of the Polynesian race. Here, we were right in the heart of what he calls the "Polynesian Triangle" and ahead, although not yet in sight, was the island of Raiatea, the "Sacred Island" to which came fleets of Polynesian vessels to join in the religious festivals, not only from Tahiti and nearby Moorea, but from the distant islands of Hawaii, the Gilberts, Marquesas and a dozen others. On such a night as this it was not difficult to imagine this fleet treading the same waters as those through which we were now passing; great ships of up to a hundred feet with one or more masts each rigged with its tall spritsail, the twin hulls (hewn from the trunks of great trees and planked up to increase their free-board) and on the deck between them the women and children asleep, the warriors eager for the first sight of land but with implicit faith in their navigators: navigators who were able to make a landfall after a voyage of two thousand miles at a time when Europe was only beginning to see the light of the Middle Ages.

It was in this mood that we first sighted Raiatea looking much bigger than it really is, with little Tahaa to the north of it. These two islands are in fact connected by a reef which encircles both as a placenta encircles twins. The wind freshened considerably and for the first time we experienced the sensation of sailing for a lee shore and a reef over which the sea tosses the spray as it breaks. We could hardly have chosen a better place on which to practise this art for not only has nature arranged two small *motus*, or islets, to flank the pass but the French have built two stone towers which, when kept in line, lead safely into the lagoon. We rounded to and made fast to the quay at the village of Uturoa.

This happy place was full of light and movement. Swift sailing pirogues (Robinson says they are the fastest in the world) sped across the lagoon, their outriggers lifting to windward in the sharper squalls, larger craft came in from Tahaa laden with fruit, the women in bright dresses, the sun shining on the greens and purples of the shallows, and at no great distance the Pacific breaking on the endless reef that keeps the water between the islands smooth.

Over this paradise presides the French Administrator M. René Charnay, and it was to his house that we went that afternoon. He came to the door. At first he seemed far from cordial, but this was due to a misunderstanding about our nationality. He showed us into a spacious room overlooking the harbour, and at once my eye was caught by the head of a Tahitian girl superbly sculpted in stone; the work of his wife, who was now waiting at Papeete for the birth of her child.

At first René Charnay's sidewhiskers and fringe of beard round the perimeter of his chin, together with his signature "rené charnay" gave him rather a precious look, but this was an impression that was soon forgotten when he started to speak. Although he was still a young man his life had been more adventuresome than many. He had finished reading Law at the Sorbonne (paying for it by working at night at an abattoir) and during the War he had been extremely active in the Resistance. He entered the Colonial Service and was sent as District Commissioner to French Gambier. From his description this sounded as primitive a place as you could find in the world of today, and he had had the unusual experience of having to shoot three of his natives for eating their wives. He must have won their confidence before he left, because he was made a member of a secret society to which no white man had been previously admitted. At his initiation he was given a small, beautifully carved box that contained a red, odourless powder. This he was told to guard with his life, because it killed without leaving a trace. Later he had it analysed by a friend in Paris who confirmed that it was extremely lethal, nor could he say what the poison was.

"Did you keep it?" I asked.

"Of course," he replied. "After all, one never knows."

There was a little restaurant near the quay owned by a Marseillais to which he took us for dinner. There were benches round wooden tables, and on these we sat eating Polynesian food garnished by the resources of the Midi and washed down by a wine of Burgundy. Our conversation, I kept thinking, was the sort of talk which you might listen to anywhere in France, with its peculiar detachment towards the disasters, the history and the future of their country that only Frenchmen acquire. In the background came the haunting note of Tahitian songs, the soft shuffle of bare feet dancing. For a moment M. Charnay listened; then, with a little grimace, half comic, half sad, he cried, "Why should we be so cruel and want to make these children grow up?'

The day we left Raiatea there occurred one of those small happenings which only take on their proper significance when viewed in the light of later events. The channel across the lagoon splits round Le Banc Central. The tide was low and the wind ahead. Anne went up to con the ship, for in places there would be little room for the short tacks we should have to make.

We had covered only a short distance when she called down, "I don't see a way through. We must turn back."

Knowing the place only from the chart I started to reassure her, but she climbed down and came aft.

"It's too far from home to take risks," she said.

It was so unlike her not to enjoy such a simple puzzle for so experienced a pilot that for a moment her words disturbed me, but later she seemed to have recovered, and I put off trying, as I so often do, to answer such awkward questions.

That evening we sailed into Apu Bay on Tahaa, and in the short dusk we rowed into a sort of inland lake. The woods, the smoke curling up into the still air from the native huts, reminded us of Friday Street near Leith Hill.

"I wish we were there," said Anne. "I wonder whether I shall ever see it again."

To Borabora or as it was once known "Porapora of the muffled paddles" was a matter of sixteen miles, but it was a sail to remember. The reef off the south-western aspect of the island is a mile wide. A low muttering, like thunder over distant hills, only continuous and infinitely sinister, great seas rising like lions to the kill, their white manes toppling, the green shallow water over the reef, the whole scene dominated by Temanu whose rocky slabs look like an old time locomotive in a wild west film. We raced in through Teavanui (the only pass in this immense barrier) under a press of sail. As Anne stood on the ratlines conning her in I was reminded of Mr Charles Pears's painting, *The Clerk's Dream*. It was all here in front of my eyes, with us in place of the schooner.

A passing pirogue pointed us round to Faanui bay to tie up alongside a concrete wall built by the Americans during the war. We had had a full day, so it seemed to us, but it was by no means over. By the time we had finished our meal a little crowd had collected and, curious at the sight of a man doing the washing-up, they had come aboard to investigate more closely; then, taking us lightly by the hand, girls for the men and a man for Anne, they led us through the forest towards the beat of drums. We came to a clearing lit by flares, and there were two lines of women sitting on their haunches performing the breadfruit dance under the *Chef de hula*. No conductor could have expressed more clearly what he thought of his orchestra than did this man of his pupils. His eyes flashed at a break in the rhythm, he danced with rage at a careless movement, he clapped at a graceful gesture, taking his class back and over till their movements were all but perfect. This team, at the Carnival, carried all before them. Well done, *Chef de hula*!

By the quay at the little village of Vaitape stands, on a plinth, the bust of Alain Gerbault. No man since Paul Gauguin died had so goaded and jibed at authority for its exploitation of the natives, nor had anyone more enjoyed the goading. Alain Gerbault, after his world voyage in *Firecrest*, had become a national figure and on his return to Tahiti the Governor with his retinue came down to the quay to welcome him. Gerbault was on deck. He waited till the Governor started his speech and then deliberately turned his back and disappeared down the hatch, slamming it after him. The bust shows an arrogant, sensitive face, more artist than seaman.

The days passed quickly. Taihuto lent us bicycles when we wanted to go to the village, we rowed round the southern end of the island where the colours on the reef and on the *motus* are beyond my powers to describe, and we had a visit from François Sandford, the schoolmaster. François' grandfather came from Boston, his mother was half French, half Tahitian, but he himself is passionately Tahitian.

"What is the good of my teaching these children French history?" he asked, "when all they want to know about is their own country. If I taught them how to be better fishermen, or to grow more taro and breadfruit, I should be doing something useful."

He had started a pamplemousse plantation and children took cuttings from his trees so that one day they would have plantations of their own.

We were asked to dinner with the Sandfords one night. The weather was stormy and the rain came down in sheets. As we were gloomily contemplating the mile-long walk there was a sound of an engine, and there was François in a battered old truck, the only vehicle we ever saw on the island. He drove us through the steaming forest over a road that was now a lake while the rain drummed down on the roof as it did in the story by Mr Somerset Maugham. Lysa Sandford stood on her veranda to welcome us. The mother of six children, she had a slender and willowy figure, and her head reminded me of the sculptured girl in M. Charnay's drawing-room. Lysa, like her husband, had the blood of more than one race in her veins, but was as proudly Tahitian as he.

After dinner I was looking through their scrap-book when I came across a letter from President Roosevelt thanking François, as *Agent français* for his discretion and tact during the occupation of the island by six thousand American troops. It had not been easy.

One night, at a dinner party to which the Sandfords had been invited, a Colonel, who had looked on the wine when it was red, insisted that Lysa should drink from his glass. She refused. The Colonel rose to his feet and hurled the glass out of the open window. Lysa, shaking with fury, stood facing him and a sudden hush fell on the noisy scene. Slowly a smile crept over the Colonel's face.

"Guess I made a fool of myself, Lysa. Let's sit down and forget it."

François liked the Americans. He could appreciate their big-heartedness and the way they wrote to him year after year at Christmas, as if the friendship formed during those years mattered to them.

Sometimes when we were shifting stores or working on the rigging or touching up paintwork I would find that Anne had slipped away for a little to talk to Mati, Taihuto's wife, while she prepared the huge bowl of manioc and taro on which the family seemed to live, or busied herself making grass skirts and costumes for the Carnival at Tahiti. She and Taihuto used to come and sit in our cabin bringing an egg or a papaw, and I treated Taihuto's leg. After a week we felt we could have stayed there for ever. There was a tranquillity about it, a restfulness of spirit like the Peace of God.

CHAPTER NINE

IN THE WAKE OF THE GREAT CANOES

HONOLULU, to which port we were now bound, lies a little west of Borabora and not much more than two thousand two hundred miles to the north of it, but to get there in a sailing ship the *Ocean-Passages of the World* (as inspiring to me as the *Odyssey* to the ancient Greeks), suggests making to the east-ward to cross the "Line" on the hundred and forty-seventh meridian of longitude. This deviation, adding several hundred miles to a voyage that is already long enough, is necessary for two distinct and separate reasons; the adverse direction of the North Pacific Trade Wind and the westward-flowing equatorial currents.

There is, it is true, a ribbon of east-going current between the broad layers of the north and south equatorial streams but this counter-current, as it is called, is unreliable and has even been known not to flow at all. So the thing to do, I thought, was to sail a point free while we were still within the influence of the South-East Trades, keeping the wind on the starboard bow as the Hawaiians had done when returning from the festivals and feasts at Raiatea nearly a thousand years ago.

Although the morning of our departure was ushered in by rain and by wind blowing at nearly gale force, the weather cleared during the day, and, by the time we were ready to be cast off from the quay by the little group of people who had come to say good-bye, it could hardly have been more fair. Sailing along the outside of the reef in smooth water, with the sun shining on the *motus*, the beaches, the verdant forest and the chuckling sea, it would have taken little to make us turn back; but then who could tell if we should ever be able to bring ourselves to leave again?

By the time we had rounded the northern end of the island the past had slipped away like a dream and we were pitching into a head sea, leaning over at the uncomfortable angle of a ship hard on the wind. Having sailed downhill, so to speak, for ten thousand miles none of us was looking forward to the sudden lurch, the buffeting, the quick cling with the hand, the crazy angle of the drinking mug and, worse than all, the damp, stifling heat below when the forehatch has to be kept tightly shut. In a big sea we either stuff a sail between the pram and the cabin top and cut down the light or else run the risk of spray coming in through the closed skylight as if it wasn't there. As we are more cheerful in the light we usually wait until one bunk or the other is soaked through before applying the remedy, as with the horse and the stable door. And all this we had exchanged for the long, easy roll with the steady Trade Wind blowing through the cabin and the forehatch open to the sky. No wonder people run round the world!

By the time dinner was over it looked as if we were in for a dirty night. The washing-up bowl, canted to stop most of the greasy water from slopping on to the floor, was between my feet, the plates stacked in one deep tray ready to be put into the other when they were dry. Every now and then a bucketful of water would come down the hawse-pipe for as yet Anne had been unable to find the tennis ball with which she usually plugged it up. Plasticine, her second line of defence, had not proved entirely efficient, for half-an-inch of water was lapping over the fo'c'sle floor. Tennis balls and plasticine! Shades of Gilbert's First Sea Lord!

I looked out into the inky blackness of the night to where the binnacle light shone dimly on Christopher's face, and even as I looked he called for a second reef. I waved my hand to show I'd heard, but I went on with the washing-up hoping I'd finish it like Drake his rubber of bowls, but a moment later we must have dived into quite a biggish sea, for a large part of it, so it seemed to me, came through the closed skylight as I knew it would if we waited long enough. I handed the mop to Anne and went up to help Christopher reef.

When I came down again the floor was washed, everything stowed away, the bunks smoothed under the waterproof covers that we clip on over our harbour ones, the tennis ball found and Anne sitting curled up in her corner writing her diary as if this was the most natural way to make a journey. By now it

5

was almost ten o'clock. Backing the foresail a little towards the mast we left *Moonraker* to plunge through the night while we slept uneasily below. So adaptable are even the more frail of the human race that after a couple of days of this we had almost forgotten what running before the wind was like.

Fourteen days and eleven hundred miles after leaving Bora-bora we crossed the "Line" on the meridian of 145° 30° W. I had had a bad throat, and it was unfortunate that this coincided with the worst night of the passage. Sweating with fever and aching from head to foot I listened to the creaking and groaning of the labouring ship and the note of the wind in the rigging. She wanted another reef. Was Anne asleep? Ought I to call her or was the weather not as bad as I thought?

Then I saw her get up, wake Christopher, heard the sounds of their going on deck, the wild flapping of the mainsail until they pulled down the clue, Anne's voice, shrill against the wind, Christopher's answering shout. In the morning Anne said, "We had quite a night; finished up with three reefs and the small jib."

"I didn't hear a thing," I said.

The wind, after heading us for several days, had again settled in the south-east and on the night in question (we were due to cross the "Line" at midnight) the ship was running with the sheets well eased for the first time on this voyage, course having been altered to north after noon that day. The night was very fine, the moon was up, the sea smooth and small Trade Wind clouds drifted across the sky. I was writing up my log before relieving Christopher, when he called down:

"Peter! There's a flare on the starboard bow!"

By the time I was up it had gone.

"What was its bearing?"

"About north by east."

"Was it going up when you first saw it, or down?"

"I think up, but I can't be sure."

"How far away?"

"I've no idea, but not close."

From the crosstrees I looked out on the blue-black ocean, the silvery bow wave as *Moonraker* sailed through the night, and from a few feet below Anne watched too. Could it have been a flare from a boat? It was more likely, I thought, for it to have come from an aircraft a hundred miles away, but always at the back of one's mind was the thought of some ship's boat or a yacht with no more flares to send.

Three days later the South-East Trades left us at the southern edge of the Doldrums as if the wind had come to a fence beyond which it dare not blow. This belt of squalls, calms and torrential rains lies between the South-East and the North-East Trades and varies in width from a hundred and fifty miles to several hundred according to the longitude you are in, the season of the year and even the year itself. Huge rain-filled clouds hung in the sky, winds came from all points of the compass, and for hours we lay on a glassy sea. To catch every breath, each sail had to be constantly trimmed, and we hung grimly on to the topsail and genoa even when a squall hummed in the rigging and water hissed over the lee deck. We shivered with cold in the rain and steamed in the pitiless sun.

After three days Anne's throat became so painful with a double quinsy that she couldn't swallow at all. I put her to bed and started her on penicillin, but she got worse instead of better. Before my eyes she developed signs of blood-poisoning, and in the middle of that night the wind struck from the north-north-east with a whoop of glee. Have you ever tried to nurse a patient with a temperature of 104° in a small boat close-hauled to a Force 5 wind?

In time, that seemed like years, her temperature started to fall, and with another half-dozen injections she should be well. I went to my case for my last box. Instead of twelve doses, there were three! But in a sailing ship you must either be dead or well and it was only five days later that Anne crept back on watch.

The rest of our passage to Oahu, the island on which Honolulu stands, was pure joy. The wind went round to east-north-east and our course trended more to the west. The bracing wind, the perfect weather put colour in Anne's cheeks. We sailed to windward of the island of Hawaii with its tremendous mountain (they say it blankets the Trade for a hundred miles) and it was a poor day when the ship's run was less than 125 miles.

On the thirtieth day out, soon after dark, we saw the lights of Hilo twenty miles to the south. The wind increased and in the morning Maui was abeam. As we ran into the Palolo Channel the wind became much stronger. I was on deck at the time, partly because I like looking at the land after a month at sea and partly because of the weather, when behind Christopher's back I saw a cloud, yellowy white, a twisting, writhing thing, advance with the speed of an express train, turning the water to steam. Thank heavens for our small spinnaker! I lowered the halyard a couple of feet, jerked the jaws of the spar away from the mast, and in ten seconds the sail was down, blanketed by the mainsail. The squall struck; the mast bent, the bows went down and down until the bow-wave came over the stem, the gear creaked and groaned but, much to my surprise, it held. Five minutes later the worst was over. We tucked in another reef.

Squalls of gale force, calms, light airs and a pitch dark night under the lee of Molokai, great tugs towing huge pineapple barges (some trick of the light made them look like railway carriages), and just before dawn out into the Kaiwi Channel with the island of Oahu dimly visible in the lightening sky, its roughened peaks running down the northern side like the spines of a prehistoric monster.

At close quarters all semblance to a South Sea island vanished. Masses of low-slung bungalows, never-ending processions of cars (like torpedoes in cream and red and green), huge pink palaces in which no prince would ever reign, tall, modern buildings, fun-fairs and enormous flags proclaimed the might of the U.S.A. which has swept the Polynesian race from off the face of this island all for the sake of "progress".

As we beat into the narrow entrance of the main harbour a ketch overhauled us, her crew waving and shouting to attract our attention. At last, for our thoughts were far away, we recognized the crew of *Ghost* (whom we had met at Tahiti) among the crowd on deck.

We were, apparently, going into quite the wrong place and

they had most kindly come out to put us right, piloting us into the Alomoana Yacht Basin. Here we were manœuvred into a pen (like one of those double-ended cars) and left to the Customs and Immigration. The Harbour Master came to welcome us. "Say, Captain," he said, "I'm sure glad to know you. Would you like for me to plug in the power and the telephone?"

Before we could step ashore the Ghosts came back. *Ghost* was much slighter than *Moonie*, although she was a foot or two longer. She had been designed by a well-known Auckland yacht-designer and had done extremely well in some of the Tasman races. There were four Ghosts, the owner Ken, a stevedore and a racing bicyclist, Neil the navigator, and his elder brother Keith, a truck-driver, and Arnold, who was a fireman in Auckland. After eighteen months' work (or was it two years?) these four had saved up enough money to take six months off and see something of the world. This sort of thing is by no means exceptional in New Zealand, although *Ghost* was smaller than most of the boats that set out on the edge of the Roaring Forties to make their easting before sailing north to the South Sea Islands. What seemed remarkable to us was that four men, none of them small, were able to live at peace with each other in such very confined quarters. Perhaps it was because they did not make the mistake of staying too long in port, and while at sea they drove their ship to the limit as if they were in an ocean race.

While we had been at Papeete, Neil and I, as navigators will, had been discussing our routes across the oceans, and Neil had seen my track (of which I was not in the least proud) across the South Pacific.

He said, "Good Lord, Peter, surely you don't bother to take sights every day when you're in the middle of the ocean?"

I murmured that I indeed did do so, not only to find the ship's position at least once in the twenty-four hours, but because knowing the day's run was good for the ship's morale; it made each man do his best to make the next one better.

"Oh," said Neil, "I only take mine once a week until I get near my landfall."

We asked what sort of a trip they'd had coming up from the Marquesas and how long had it taken.

Ken, in an off-hand sort of way said, "It took us thirty-two days."

The others laughed.

"Come on, Neil," said Arnold. "Spill the beans."

And, with a rueful grin Neil began his story. They had made good time, he said, up to the "Line" and through the Doldrum belt. He had been taking the ship's position once a week as was his custom until within three hundred miles of Hawaii, when he had intended to take it every day. It was most unfortunate (but just the sort of thing that happens) that the weather at this time was unusually bad for these parts and that the sun's angle at mid-day was over 80°, so that he had to take the sun's meridian altitude exactly at noon to find his latitude. But the sun did not come out at noon. And on the second and third days the sun did not come out at noon. By now he was getting a little worried. He had been able to get a longitude position line that put him on the longitude of Oahu and he was still sure that he was south of the island. "There's nothing to worry about," he said to Ken. "Steer north and you'll sight the island in the morning." When morning came there was no island but that day the sun came out at noon and Neil took his sight. They were two hundred miles north of Oahu still steering north, and the next land ahead was the Alaskan Peninsula!

CHAPTER TEN

HONOLULU

HONOLULU . . . a vast hotel, a crowd of smart women, men with open-necked shirts imprinted with the forty-eight States of the Union, attentive waiters, a lift soaring to unknown heights, an endless corridor with doors discreetly labelled: doctors, attorneys-at-law, real estate and the British Consulate (like cells in some Utopian prison): a friendly drugstore (air-conditioned like the rest), where people understand the problems of small boats, a place to linger over a malted milk shake; a window where native carving is beautifully displayed and costs the earth; streets jammed with cars (more cars than people), and red and cream buses tearing up the long, straight, hot road back to the Alamoana Yacht basin, a road along which no bicycle and no pedestrian ever passes. An island thick with wealth and the high standard of living, where *hula* dances are organized by kind permission of Kodak; an island with the most perfect climate in the world, on whose northern coast the Pacific thunders in almost primeval state, whose coral sands still lie virgin on Sunset Beach, whose every available acre is used for the growing of pineapple, whose mountain ridge (sharp as a razor's edge) is pierced by a narrow gap, through which the Trade Wind roars with such violence that it blows a waterfall upwards: an island possessing the finest museum of Polynesian art and history in the Pacific, through whose doors we dare not penetrate, for it is easier for us to enjoy this place if we think of it as pure American.

We had introductions to several families living here, and the first one we made contact with asked us to a party two days later.

Our hostess graciously agreed to come and see our ship before driving us back to the house, and we were at some pains to be sure we recognized her before she should get lost among the vast numbers of vessels in the basin. We had no difficulty. As she advanced along the wooden staging, her stately bearing, the small parasol above her head, her daughter and two grand-children walking just the right distance behind her, removed all doubts from our minds that this was our distinguished visitor. Tall, and with a face not unlike that of the late Queen Mary, she stood looking at our boat, and I could see that she was filled with wonderment that any friend of hers could have written introducing such a vessel's complement. She accepted the situation and summoned sufficient courage to climb down the companionway into the cabin. Here she refused an invitation to sit down, but remained standing under the skylight (the only place where this was possible), her eyes wandering shrewdly from corner to crevice, and we were thankful to have had time to make the place as presentable as any cabin in a small ship engaged on a deep-water voyage can look. Anne showed her the galley (her face relaxed a little and broke into a half smile) and after that, to the disgust of her grand-children who were just starting to enjoy themselves, she said, "Now I'll take you home. There's a little more room, where we can talk."

The house was built in the Italian style, with large rooms of good height, like some of the villas I had seen overlooking Lago Maggiore. It seemed to fit in so well with the climate, the superb view over Waikiki beach and the bay beyond, that you did not question the appropriation from another country of a style so essentially traditional to it.

Our host the Senator (whose grandparents had sailed round Cape Horn and had landed on these islands among the first missionaries to come from the United States) suggested a swim in their outdoor swimming-pool and by the time we had changed back again other guests had started to arrive. This was the first American cocktail party I had ever been to, and it was a revelation after the easy, "leave you to get on with it" attitude of those in England. As far as I could see our hostess introduced everybody to everyone else with a word to explain the reason for their being there. Nor was there any need, so Christopher and I agreed, to have any dinner afterwards, for tiny steaks were provided on a spit to be dipped in delicious sauces, there were sea-foods that I had never heard about, as well as the usual sausages and whirled slivers of bacon, eggs in every form and any sort of drink you cared to ask for. Anne, poor girl, did not manage quite so well. "How can I enjoy these glorious things," she mocked, "if I have to talk to a complete stranger with my mouth full of meat and with grease on my chin?"

The party was in full swing when I noticed a small group of people coming in late. Presently I felt my arm gripped as if by a vice and, half turning, I found myself looking into a pair of sharp, bright eyes set in a pale face, of which the other remarkable feature was a thin, very firm, mouth.

"Are you Dr Pye?" and as I moved my lips, he went on, "I'm Dick Rheem of the *Morning Star* (an ocean racer, not a newspaper). You gave me the shock of my life."

Seeing the puzzled look on my face he laughed. "There was I, last Thursday, rounding into the Kaiwi Channel, knowing I was first or second boat in (and we'd done pretty well, I figured) when what d'you think I saw, fine on my port bow? A miserable little reefed down gaff cutter!"

We had, I remembered, glimpsed a large ocean racer coming in from the sea, and we'd wondered whether she was one of the Trans-Pacific fleet on the last lap of their 2,150-mile passage from San Pedro. But she'd passed us long before we came to Diamond Head.

I said, "She looked a beauty."

"No good trying to talk about boats here," he said with a wry grin. "Come aboard tomorrow morning."

And at that moment we both became involved once more in the meshes of conviviality.

The *Morning Star* was a bermudian ketch ninety-eight feet long. Her sheer was a delight to a sailor's eye and, unusual in a modern yacht, she was distinctly rakish. She had been rigged as a schooner and had established an all-time record from San Pedro to Diamond Head of nine-and-a-half knots. After an accidental gybe in the middle of a wildish night Dick Rheem could never quite forget how much worse it might have been and had her converted into a ketch at the cost, it was con- fidently rumoured, of a hundred "grand". Now ships, like

women, sometimes have an aura round them; some are just
plain dull, others have the spice of life, while some you take
your cap off to and offer up a silent prayer, but if Dick had
said, "What about a voyage around the Horn?" I'd have left
with him that morning.

Our host appeared on deck. He was an American version of
an Elizabethan and his voice (I only heard him raise it once)
could put a "jump into a wooden dog". *Morning Star* carried a
racing crew of sixteen men. Dick said, "I don't ever have any
trouble with 'em. If they can't discipline themselves they
don't come aboard twice."

Before we left he said, "Connie and I (Connie, his wife had,
like most of the other wives, flown over to join her husband)
want you all to come to the *Morning Star* party on Wednesday."

That very day Anne went down with a bad throat and a
temperature. Feeling anything but in the right sort of party
mind I followed Christopher into the Royal Hawaiian Hotel.
I had heard so much about this place that I probably expected a carpet of gold to be surrounded by the spices of the
Orient, so I was faintly disappointed to find that it was nothing
more than a good, high-class hotel. We gathered for the cocktail party in a large private room which was soon crammed
with people. Andy, a sailor and a composer of songs, made a
speech and handed round copies of a song that he had written
especially for the occasion. I sing it still for it has a catchy little
tune.

We went in to lunch. I can recollect little of the conversation between my neighbours and myself for its details were
lost in a background of tremendous sound, of enormous, exu-
berant vitality against which the songs of three Hawaiian
minstrels were submerged, their mouths moving to inaudible
words. Facing me, between the pillars of the building, was the
beach and the reef beyond which the jade seas rolled in, the
spray whipped from their crests by the off-shore wind like
snow from the ridge of a mountain. I gazed at this scene in all
its brilliant colouring, my mind puzzled by the feeling that
there was something missing. Then my fuddled brain woke

up. There was no sound as the breakers fell; their roar was drowned by the clamour within.

Dick Rheem drove me back to the Yacht Basin, and as we said good-bye (he and Connie were leaving in the morning by air for San Francisco) he handed me a deep red *lei* for Anne. He said, "You're doing what I should like to do but it looks as if time will never let me catch up with it. Good sailing, and come and see us in San Francisco."

I found Anne's temperature higher and her throat worse. Although massive doses of penicillin soon put her right, I made up my mind from this moment that we must spend the winter in British Columbia. It was not only that by the time we reached Victoria we should have sailed twelve thousand miles in seven months, but it was the constant change of scene, meeting new people and absorbing so many different impressions that had worn Anne out. Once again we had received a warm invitation from Beryl Smeeton, and even if we didn't spend the winter in her house we could always live on the boat.

When I talked to Christopher he said, "Apart from Anne's illness I don't think we could have gone on. I feel, quite badly, that I need a spell ashore. I'll write to my parents; they may want me to go home."

We had meant to spend only a week at Honolulu, but when Anne was better one party led so easily to another, and Christopher was having the time of his life. There was a great deal to do to the ship. We changed over from our light tropical mainsail to our 18-oz. northern waters sail, and we renewed the running gear that we had been unable to replace at Tahiti because it was so expensive and of such poor quality. Here, it was cheaper than in England. The copper on the starboard side at the waterline was as thin as paper and was peeling off a foot at a time between the bows and the shrouds. Ernie Simmerer, who was a naval architect as well as doing shipwright work, said he thought he could find some copper that wouldn't cost much and that he would help me to put it on. But by then I had come to know Ernie fairly well. He had made a ratline for me, and when I went to pay for it he said, "Someone gave me this bit of oak and I made it while I was talking business to a client. It hasn't cost me a cent, so it won't cost you anything, either."

Rumour had it that Ernie wasn't doing very well, which is hardly to be wondered at, for he rebuilt a mast for an Australian ketch that had been dismasted three hundred miles to the south of Oahu, where her owner and his wife, both past middle age, rigged a jury one and made port. He refused to let them have a bill "because they did such a fine job".

I said firmly, "Ernie, there's another layer of copper under that one and it's going to last us back to England."

We had been in the basin only a very short time when the Crowes came to see us. We had met them in their schooner *Lang Syne* in 1950 sailing down Sir Francis Drake's Channel in the Virgin Islands; and later in the island of St. Thomas. They had completed their three-year circumnavigation of the world and were now living on their ship in the basin. Bill ran the slipway, and Billie his wife, worked in a store; one day, when they had gathered together a sufficient reserve, they hoped to sail again. *Lang Syne* was stripped of gear and sails, but her great beam gave the impression below that you were in a small house. When I came into the saloon (Billie now called it the "living-room") three things caught my eye. A carved spear from the Marquesas, given them by Bob McKitterick when they beat back eight hundred miles with something he badly needed from Tahiti, the carved head of a girl from Bali and a painting by Le Tec, a Frenchman who had been killed in an accident shortly before we arrived at Papeete, a man who used black velvet instead of canvas. René Charnay dubbed him a charlatan, the Americans raved about him. This was a painting of a Tahitian drummer. His head was thrown back and his face was alight with a pagan ecstasy. It reminded me of the sketch of the head of "the Soldier" by Leonardo da Vinci and the sheen on that native's arms shone like the painting of a velvet gown by David Jagger.

Bill said, "I knew Le Tec (he pronounced it Lee Tagg) quite well. He was down and out and wanted money to buy more drink. I gave him sixty dollars. A guy offered me six thousand the other day, but I wouldn't part with it, not for all the tea in China."

Bill and I discussed our passage to Victoria. He said, "The rule is, make easting if you can and northing if you must"; but I had noticed from the American wind charts that north of 45° N. the winds were north of north-west, so I proposed to sail due north for 1,500 miles before turning towards the east. By doing this I hoped (I might almost say I prayed) that the worst of the Pacific "High" (where we might be becalmed for days or weeks) would lie on my starboard hand.

On the Canadian yacht Dragoon (fifty-nine feet long and the only British entry in the Trans-Pacific race) the "High" was plotted every day and, as their departure, and ours, grew nearer, they plotted it every hour. As the centre may move to a spot five hundred miles away as easily as a flea jumps into a bed, all this seemed to us to be only faintly profitable to a vessel sailing a hundred miles a day. When we left Captain Holmes, R.C.N., wished us good-bye.

"We leave tomorrow," he said. "I'll give you a bottle of whisky if you get there first."

CHAPTER ELEVEN

THE SUN SHINING ON A GLACIER

NORTH of 45° N. the Pacific is a gloomy sea, said to be the most sunless of the oceans of the world. The crew of *Gemini* (an American couple who roam the world as Arabs roam the desert) told us that we would have the utmost difficulty in getting sights and that during the summer months the coastline of Vancouver Island and the State of Washington to the south of it were usually enshrouded in mist or fog. The winds, we hoped, would be fresh and aft of the beam, for the stronger they were the quicker should we arrive at our destination.

Towards this sunless sea we sailed from Honolulu on a Thursday in July making our way to the westward under the lee of the land. It was almost dark by the time Point Kaena came in sight but fierce squalls already warned us of what lay ahead. Dinner was eaten hurriedly, the dishes stowed away, and a second reef tucked in the mainsail. Taking a deep breath, we rounded the Point.

Bill Crowe, when talking of our departure had said, "Oh, boy; oh, boy, those first three hundred miles will sure be rugged." And Bill was right. In a matter of a minute or two we were soaked to the skin by the sheets of spray driven across our decks from the steep and vicious seas. Slamming the hatch behind us, we went below leaving old *Moonie* to fight this battle on her own, close-hauled on the starboard tack.

Blear-eyed and weary, for it had been almost as wet and wild below as above, I went up on deck at six o'clock the next morning. It was still blowing hard, but the seas had lengthened out, and a glance aloft showed that all was well. Oahu was out of sight astern, and the discomforts of such a night had, I thought, one compensation. If the ship had survived them she was unlikely to fall apart in the immediate future; for she was then fifty-eight years old, eighteen years beyond the age when Mr Humphrey Barton thinks that a yacht has finished her ocean-going days. Although we had kept her up to the best of our (and King's) ability, her underwater body was as it had been when we bought her twenty-two years ago, except for some added fastenings.

Weeks afterwards, we were told that *Dragoon*, sailing twenty-four hours after us, had had her troubles too. Driving through the darkness she had carried away a forestay, lost a sail and had had to be pumped out in the middle of the night. The crew had said, "What about poor old *Moonie*; d'you think she's still afloat?"

Sailing six points off the wind we covered 312 miles in three days, and on the fourth we shot out of the Trade Wind belt as if it were a line of demarcation across the ocean. Lying idly upon the sea waiting for a breeze we saw a steamer hull down on the southern horizon. To our astonishment she turned and headed in our direction and presently came abreast of us. Her captain, using the loud hailer, called:

"Are you all right?" in a thick Norwegian accent.

"Yes," I answered and then thanked him for coming all this way to find out. Without another word, the captain swung her round and continued on his way. So odd was this abrupt breaking off of relations (for ship's masters are seldom business-like when talking to small boats in the middle of large oceans) that we cast about for some explanation. Christopher, I think, found the most likely one. "Our mainsail is red," he argued, "the same colour as that of a ship's lifeboat. I suppose he was upset when he found she was only a miserable yacht in no trouble at all."

Followed a week of perfect sailing, seven hundred miles in seven days with hardly a sheet started except to follow the wind as it veered from east to south. On the twelfth night out a sub-tropical sunset of unusual warmth seemed to promise that these conditions would hold, but by morning the scene had changed with the speed of a moving picture. The temperature dropped like a stone; two jerseys, a flannel shirt, heavy sea-trousers and long sea-boots replaced the shorts and singlet. The veiled sky and the long brownish wisps of cloud (my "cohorts" of an advancing depression) were there waiting for me.

From that moment we became alert, hard and compact; determined to drive the ship to the limit but to take no chances with this cold grey waste of sea, pitiless, watchful and waiting, so it seemed, for us to make some fatal error. The days pass. Wind and rain with scarcely a glimpse of the sun, three blankets over the watch below and plenty of good days' runs. A north-westerly gale. We heave to and sleep. I look out on a wild scene; a clearing sky, great crested seas, emerald green before they break, cold as if they'd come from the Bering Sea. A cloud advances with the speed of a train, a cloud like the hand of a man; its fingers furred by wind and stretched across the sky; a squall that makes us heave to again and drives us below to have breakfast standing within the small comfort of the Primus stove. All day we run before this strong, fair wind, the decks awash, judging the weight behind each squall. This is what we sail for, to pit our puny strength against an ocean that can crush us and send us to the bottom if it feels so inclined. Gone are the warm seas and the drying sun, but in a week we are twice the crew that we were before.

We have an air escort, self-appointed, of two North Pacific Albatrosses, locally known as Goney birds. They are brown, long-beaked and have a wing-span that looks to be about eight feet. They have been with us for a thousand miles and have made themselves extremely useful during the last two weeks by sitting on logs the size of trees which are so waterlogged that we cannot see them for more than a very short distance ahead. One at each end they sit like two towers on a breakwater, so that we cannot possibly miss them. For all we know they may sit on them at night, but in the dark we can see neither birds nor logs and simply hope that they will not lie in our path.

Our course trends away to the north-east and then east-north-east and we reach 49° N., the same latitude as the Lizard Light in Cornwall, but more like Norway at the beginning of June—now I come to think of it, even colder than that. We have one fine day when the sun comes out and it is warm, and the decks are strewn with rugs and sails and clothes, as we take this heaven-sent opportunity to dry them out. My sights

British Columbia and the Charlotte Islands

6

show that we are less than a hundred miles from Vancouver Island, and so far we have beaten our own record by sailing 2,500 miles in just under twenty-five days.

But luck is against us. An easterly gale roars at us from off the mountains that are still below the horizon, and although it blows harder than I have known it to blow at sea during all my years of sailing, the land keeps the sea from being as impressive as it would be if the direction of the wind were reversed.

Rather to my surprise the gale blows itself out from the north thirty-six hours later and at seven o'clock in the morning of the twenty-seventh day out I see the sun shining on a glacier on Mount Victoria seventy miles away. The weather changes completely. It becomes positively hot; and light winds, calm seas and wreaths of mist and fog drifting over the swell shut the land from our anxious eyes until we enter the Juan de Fuca Strait. Now it is evening and the surface of the water seems to glow with the lights of a hundred fishing boats, and the still air is filled with the hum of their high-speed engines. Dimly to starboard lies Cape Flattery, its powerful light winking in the darkness, while from the shores of Vancouver Island comes the roar of the sea on the rocks. We are contained within the boundaries of the land.

To the early explorers this strait must have seemed like the mouth of some vast whale. Seventy miles of dark and gloomy water between the Olympian range on the one hand (up to six thousand feet high) and the virgin forests and hills of Vancouver Island on the other. Where, they must have wondered, did it lead to? To the "Strait of Annan" and the "North-West Sea" or to a vortex (for the currents run strong) like a gigantic Corrievrechan from which there would be no return?

It was too much for poor Juan de Fuca, a Greek in Spanish pay, for although he probably saw the opening, the account he gave was proved so false that he could never have explored inside.

We made slow progress during the night, and in the morning wet clouds hung above the bluff to the east of Port San Juan, and only a darker grey betrayed the presence of the other side. We felt hemmed in, and the ten-mile width seemed considerably foreshortened. What a place for calms! Later, the clouds lifted and the Olympians, clear and god-like in their mantle of snow, looked down upon us, making the strait look narrower still. We were proceeding at the rate of a knot, when a ketch appeared ahead. She looked to be a vessel of about twenty tons with no sails on either mast, and with long trolling poles, like the antennae of cockroaches, lashed to her rigging. A man stepped out of the wheelhouse and joined the woman who was already standing by the rail.

"Are you the *Moonraker*?" he called. "The Smeetons have been expecting you for some days. You're late."

Although our paths did not cross again for some months this couple's story is so typical of what people do in this young and exciting country that I shall relate it as we drift, or kedge for adverse tide, on our way up the Juan de Fuca Strait. Tony was a young Canadian when war broke out. He worked his passage to England, joined the R.A.F. and, after much frustration, trained as a fighter pilot. This alone is rather surprising, for Tony is built on a massive scale, and the way he speaks and his slow and deliberate movements make you think he would be more at home in bombers. He finished up as a Squadron-Leader in night-fighters. After the war he and Bridget (a Southampton girl) married and went to Grand Cayman, where they sank all their money in having a boat built at a local yard from designs by John Alden. Her hull was hardly planked up when labour troubles broke out, so they finished the essentials themselves and sailed her up to British Columbia. The *White Hart* is what we in England call a fifty-fifty, with a small sail-plan and a large engine, but she is a superb sea-boat.

In four years of fishing they saved enough money to convert *White Hart* into a yacht and to take six months' holiday on the Californian coast. Two years later they planned a trip to New Zealand. They have a small son whose play-pen is the deck and Tony and Bridget run that ship without any help. It is a tough life; Bridget herself has caught up to three hundred fish in a day, as well as looking after her child and doing the domestic chores of a twenty-tonner. I think, too, that Tony must be an unusually good fisherman, because our friends at Fisherman's Wharf said, "All we have to do is to find Tony. That's where the fish'll be."

Only a few days ago I had a letter from Miles Smeeton saying they had met *White Hart* in mid-ocean three hundred miles south of Norfolk Island in the Tasman Sea. Tony and Bridget had loved the South Seas. Tahiti, New Zealand, British Columbia—as long as they can catch fish the world is theirs.

Three days of light airs and calms . . . but when at last we had passed Sooke Harbour a fine southerly breeze sprang up with the young spring flood. Ahead and within sight were Race Rocks and the Race Rocks Lighthouse. The Channel between the rocks and the shore is nearly a mile wide and is deep, but the surface of the water is torn by tide rips and eddies, for the current runs up to nine knots with a set towards the rocks on the flood. With this commanding wind, and with the thought in my mind that we must get used to such places I steered for the Race Rocks Passage. My crew raised their eyebrows. They did more than that; they pointed out to me that the whole of the Juan de Fuca Strait lay on my starboard hand.

The ship sailed on.

We were doing twelve knots over the ground when the wind dropped. It was as if a hand seized her, dragging her unprotesting towards those waiting fangs. Christopher went down to try the engine because, in a case like this, you must try everything. It went.

Round Williams Head we beat into the Quarantine Anchorage and came to an anchor, thirty days out from Honolulu. We should have liked to have lingered, but the doctor would have none of us. "You must be cleared by Customs tonight," he said firmly; so up went the sails once more and, like a cur chivied from one side of the street to the other, we crossed the eight-mile bay to Victoria. The sun went down lighting Mount Baker, rising above lesser peaks to a height of nearly eleven thousand feet, with alpenblum. So clear was the air that it appeared not seventy miles away as on our chart, but twenty.

It was almost dark. Fish-boats, tugs, lighters, a ferry and a forest of masts confronted us as, half blinded by the lights of harbour, ships and town, we searched for a place to lie.

Out of the maze there came a voice, "Is that *Moonraker?*" and to our despairing answer, the unknown voice shouted, "Come along in here!"

Sails came down, the ship lost way, Christopher jumped into the pram and towed us down a narrow lane between a dozen boats. Dim figures on the quay made us fast. They had seen our sails across the bay, had rung the Customs and were waiting to take us to the Harbour Office where we had to report that night. Before they left they pressed a dollar into our hands to ring the Smeetons in the morning because, they said, "You won't have any of these!"

CHAPTER TWELVE

MUSGRAVE

THERE must have been a hundred fish-boats at the wharf; large and small, with high, flaring bows and low, flat sterns, marked sheers and tall superstructures so tall as to look almost like the bridge of some larger ship, pulleys and drums, miles of wire, trolling poles slung along stumpy masts and, on the big seiners, acres of nets. Their crews were small; two men (or man and wife) to a forty-footer, and only the seiners carried more than three. Ship-to-shore radios, automatic pilots, fathometers and direction finders were standard equipment on all but the smallest.

Most of the men, it seemed, came along to look at us. Dressed in "logger's shirts" in patterns of red or yellow squares, or in thick Indian sweaters with strange birds across the front, their seaman's gait, their slow speech softened by wind and sea, nothing could have been more different from the Alamoana Basin at Honolulu.

Many of these men had emigrated, and there were others whose fathers or grandfathers had come out from the "Old Country" and were anxious to know if Bristol or Huddersfield still looked the same. Ed, who kept a bos'n's store at the head of our dock, "fixed" our broken exhaust and, on looking round, trotted back to his shop for a brand-new shackle for the bob-stay.

"That 'un you've got there looks a bit thin, Doc," he said. "You put this 'un in his place."

And then a fisherman came strolling along with a twenty-two-inch salmon dangling from his hand.

"Guess this is too small to be of any use to me," he said. "It might make a bit of a meal for you."

All this with such unconscious grace.

We rang the Smeetons. We walked along to the telephone box by Ed's shed arguing as to who should speak first because, suddenly, it had become enormously important to hear their voices.

I used the instrument.

"Hullo!" came B.'s clear voice.

"This is Peter, from Victoria."

"Peter—Peter who?"

I tried to hide my anxiety, "From England."

"Oh! Peter! Oh, my dear, where are you speaking from? When did you get in? How's Anne? What sort of a passage? Wait; I'll go and fetch Miles."

I handed over the receiver to Anne and moved around to stop my knees from shaking. By the time we'd used up the dollar we'd arranged to meet between James and Sidney Islands in the Strait of Georgia in two days' time.

From a casual acquaintance at Honolulu we had been given an introduction to a gentleman who lived outside Victoria. Very kindly, on hearing that we also knew the Smeetons, he invited us up for lunch. He was small, very light on his feet with pale eyes and a high, penetrating voice. It became obvious that he had a very full acquaintance with what might be called England's Upper Crust, and I had the impression, perhaps erroneously, that as friends of the Smeetons, we were a little undersized.

He said, sharply, "The Smeetons, although they've only been here for three or four years, have become a legend. Beryl is as tough as leather and neither of them feels the cold. The last time I was at Musgrave there were no doors or windows and I don't suppose there are any now. They probably wouldn't be considered necessary. Do you think," he questioned, "that you will be able to live that sort of life?"

"Perhaps not," I agreed, "but we can always try."

On the Wednesday morning we sailed from Victoria, negotiating the channel between Trial Island and the shore, which is less than a cable wide and where the current boils and whirls. Out in the Gulf of Georgia the wind deserted us and we settled down to a long, hot drift. A blue day; blue hills, blue mountains, blue sky, dark blue lines of breeze that never moved in our direction, so blue indeed that even the pines seemed no longer green. We lay in this idle fashion until it was borne in upon us that soon the tide would turn, so we coaxed our reluctant engine into a semblance of life (two-and-a-half knots flat out) and proceeded towards our rendezvous.

We were, of course, late; so late that *Tzu Hang* had almost given us up when she descried her long-lost sister and came bounding to meet her. The dinghy shot off her deck and B., rowing as if her life depended upon it, came alongside.

"Oh, well done, well done," she cried. "I just can't believe it."

She handed us a packet of mail, and then the two ships made their way northwards, while a steady flow of talk and news crossed and re-crossed the intervening water.

Presently Miles sang out. "We'll have to go on. I'll milk the cows and come down and put a light on Musgrave Point. You might miss it in the dark."

So they left us to thread the narrow channel of the Iroquois Pass, dodging rocky islets covered with a growth of pines, past Canoe Cove, up into Saanich Inlet and under the great bare brow of the mountain on Salt Spring Island that we were to get to know so well. A light breeze followed astern, but our thoughts, released by a temporary easing in the pilotage, took wings towards the house (marked Conspic. Ho. on the chart) which we were now approaching and to the story of how B. had found it.

Back in 1945 B., having been shown a photograph of the place, had bought it across a dinner table in India. Eighteen months later she and Clio (aged five) arrived in Eastern Canada, bought an old Canadian army truck and drove three thousand miles across Canada to Vancouver City. Taking the ferry to Salt Spring Island she covered the last four miles in as many hours over the mountain track to Musgrave.

The place was in ruins. The roof sagged, wind and weather came through the walls, the floor gave beneath their feet. B. looked round; two hundred feet below, the smooth dark water flowed towards the Sansum Narrows; across the strait rose the hills and mountains of Vancouver Island. She thought to herself, "This land, once it has been cleared, should be good for sheep and cows. Thank God Miles isn't here. He wouldn't be able to see it as I can. This is going to be worth while."

She set to work to rebuild the house, reinforced by Miles, once he had got his discharge from the Army, and then, because they were at that time unable to get their capital out of England, they ran out of money. So Miles joined the Canadian Army, was posted within the Arctic Circle in mid-winter from where he wrote letters to B. about the cold to which she replied (with undoubted truth) that she was colder than he.

In the end the Canadian Army (or the Arctic cold) gave Miles a duodenal ulcer and he returned to Musgrave and in time (a remarkably short time, it seemed to us) they had a house with a roof and walls, "country sheep" which Miles picked up cheap and left to fend for themselves in the bush, "town sheep" for which he expressed the utmost scorn (because they had to be looked after). A bull, a cow, hens, pigs, ducks, geese, guinea-fowl and a goat completed their livestock. Certain changes had been made when they came over to England to buy *Tzu Hang*; and the bull was disposed of, I had been relieved to hear, because I am not good with bulls.

It grew dark. Miles had been right about the difficulty of finding Musgrave at night. So black were the trees, and so foreshortened was the width of the water by the high ground, that I was thankful when a light, like a candle in a window, appeared from the level of the water. There was B. in a dinghy.

"Miles is standing by the buoy," she called. "Pick it up and come ashore."

By the light of a lantern we pile into the truck with a couple of kitbags with our things for the night. Then we are off. The engine roars, the wheels bite into the deep dry ruts and we head up a narrow track winding through the forest. Bumping and swaying, twigs snapping, brambles and branches brushing our faces, the warm still air, the smell of the exhaust, the scent of pines, all excite our senses. We cross a bridge over the now dry bed of a stream, a light appears among the trees, a gate that Christopher jumps down to open, the shadowy form of a house in a wide clearing. The truck turns into a shed. B. leads us through the dairy into a workroom with a high wood ceiling.

Electric saws, drills, planes, benches, an old iron stove that once heated a church, a kitchen and dining-room easy to live in and as practical as B. herself, a dishwasher, a stove that turns itself on and off, windows and doors are everywhere. The living-room is three sides of a square and in the western wing, so to speak, is the sort of fireplace you might expect in a Tudor house in England. Tibetan stirrups of carved wood, a Persian carpet found by B. on her travels, a tiger shot by Miles and a fine broad staircase leading to the bedrooms. Primitive! Why, the place is more highly mechanized than anything I'd dreamed of. We sit down to eat. I remember being surprised that five people all talking at once managed to eat so much in so short a time.

For the next three weeks we worked hard on the ship. We put her ashore and renewed the copper round the waterline, stripped her of gear and sails, scraped, varnished, painted, patched sails and counted all the tins left in our lockers of which, to our surprise, there were four hundred and seventy-five. The weather was glorious, like an Indian summer at home, and our daily walks led through the pine-woods. The forest came to the water's edge, and the cove was only open to the north, from which quarter the wind never blew with any strength.

Coming round a bend in the path we would see the masts of the two ships, the clear blue water, the Government wharf and the shed, the float and Roy's boat beside it. Fourteen feet long, beamy and flat-bottomed, I wouldn't have set foot in it on the Round Pond. Over the middle half Roy had built a high cabin to protect the tiny engine, the mail and himself, and on the front of this he had painted, in large red letters, THE ROYAL MAIL. Roy himself was thickset with a round, red face and placid eyes. He had been taught to read by one of his many uncles, had never been to school nor spent a single night away from Salt Spring Island. He spoke as his people did, with a strong Yorkshire accent. He carried the mail twice a week to and from Burgoyne Bay three miles up the coast with the determination of a King's Messenger riding across Hounslow Heath in the days of Dick Turpin. There was little he did not know about forestry and carpentry, and he adored the Smeetons, who in turn said they could overcome any catastrophe except that of losing Roy.

One morning towards the end of our refit we were working on the boat when there came the sound of a hunting horn and when we looked up we saw a ship that was suddenly familiar to us. She was the *Tara*. She belonged to an engineer from San Pedro and it was he who had taken us through the passage in the reef to the Alamoana basin in Honolulu. At the time Bill had said he might be going to Alaska and we had suggested he should call in on his way south. They had come down from Ketchikan by the "Inside Passage" delighted with their ship and excited at the success of their voyage. Miles was down in the cove that afternoon and we all went aboard. *Tara* was about thirty-six feet along, very beamy and of moderate draught, and it was astonishing to me that Bill could have built her himself in four years working only during holidays and at week-ends. There was, however, one thing we didn't quite like. The main gaff went up and down on a steel jackstay. It seemed to us to be not quite strong enough to take the strain of that swinging spar.

Bill and his wife and their two friends were invited up to baths and dinner at the house and we sat yarning over the fire as sailors will.

Miles asked Bill if he had had any trouble with his gaff, to which Bill replied, "None at all. If it comes on to blow I lower my main and turn on the engine."

I must have murmured something about a lee-shore for I remember Bill saying, "I can't imagine a sea so big that I couldn't motor into it."

Tara left the next morning bound for Seattle and then for San Francisco. Two weeks later we heard there had been bad weather on the west coast, and we wondered how *Tara* had fared, but it was a long time before we were to hear what happened.

The work on *Moonraker* finished, Christopher went off to Victoria to become a plumber's mate in a shipyard at seventy dollars a week. Before he went he drew me aside to tell me he'd heard from his people (as we had done) that they were anxious for him to finish the voyage back to England.

"And of course," he added, "I want to, too."

Until that moment I had been almost certain that he would leave us, and I wondered at what stage during the passage north he had changed his mind. And how like him not to come bursting down with the news at the end of some nautical crisis (as I should have done), but to have waited patiently until he was absolutely certain. Well; we should be delighted.

So Christopher went off to live at Fisherman's Wharf, and before we laid the ship up for the winter we sailed down to find him living on tins of Chuck Waggon Dinner and Pacific Milk and sharing a houseboat, sleeping in the owner's bunk by day and working by night.

It was blowing hard, very hard in the Juan de Fuca Strait the day we said good-bye to him, but under the lee of Vancouver Island we had no more difficulty than tying several reefs in the mainsail. We arrived so late at Musgrave that we spent the night aboard and walked up to Conspic. Ho. in the morning.

Beryl said; "Christopher rang twice last night to ask whether you were back. He sounded as anxious as if he'd been your son."

Looking back on the six months that we spent at Musgrave it seems to fall into two parts like the two acts of a short play; the autumn and the winter. Part of the plan for the autumn was that we should look after the farm whenever the Smeetons went away for a few days, so Anne and I were shown how to milk. We started by milking one cow between us, for Anne's hands being smaller she found it easier to milk from the front teats while I tried the back. Our wrists ached, Folly put her foot in the bucket and Molly seemed to have dried right up.

Miles, when asked how we were getting on, said, "Peter gets the best results but Anne has the better style."

At the end of a week Anne headed her diary, "I Milk a Whole Cow". Miles showed me how to split logs, to use the machinery in the workroom, and Anne was taken along by B. to feed the animals, but most of the day I spent writing down on the boat trying to earn some dollars before starting off in the spring.

Anne worked at the house in the mornings, came down to the boat to help me in the afternoons and cooked the dinner at the house in the evenings. When the Smeetons were away I usually milked the cows and she fed the animals.

B. ran her house as Anne runs *Moonraker* on a long sea voyage—no waste, no frills but plenty of the essentials. One plate, one knife and two hot meals a day. To this sort of thing we took like ducks to water, for we were used to it. Nothing but flour, sugar and rice was brought in from the outside world except a sack of potatoes which, in a weak moment, B. got for the Pyes, when their faces fell at the thought of six months of rice. The day started with porridge cooked with milk instead of water in a double saucepan. I asked B. where she had learned to make it that way.

"I was living on a ranch in Patagonia," she said, "and one day I stupidly got lost whilst out riding. After a day and a night I came on an Indian family camping and they fed me on this. It tasted like ambrosia, and I've made it this way ever since."

Porridge and cream and eggs, and cup after cup of coffee; but how B. mattocked all day in the bush on two slices of charred toast (for that was all she ever had) I cannot think. It was her boast that she could sit down and eat for an hour or two on end and last the next thirty-six without another bite. I can believe her.

If you felt weak in the middle of the day you could always gnaw bread and drink milk, and while we were there tea and cake round the workroom fire after dark became an institution that even B. recognized. Twice a week she baked bread, delicious brown loaves, the best I've ever tasted, but once when she and Anne were gossiping away together she forgot to put in the yeast. Thinking that yeast late was better than never she threw some in, with the result that each loaf could have replaced a sizeable pig of our ballast. Those loaves looked like lasting a long time, until I hit on the idea of taking a new one down to the boat each day. None came back, and B. only got wise to my sudden extravagance after I had put the last of them into my bag. I fled down the path.

I became the unofficial doctor to the few inhabitants on that part of the island, a Dutch family near the Smeetons and the various branches of the Smith family of which Roy was one. Koos and his wife had spent their early married life on a barge on a Dutch canal. His prospects of getting on, said Koos, seemed nil when he received a letter from America offering him (through a Dutch friend) the job of caretaker to the American's house above Musgrave Cove. Koos was the right man for the post; a tremendous worker and always good-tempered, he had saved money, had a little farm of his own and two children one of whom I had to see fairly often. As often as not I returned to Musgrave with a bagful of greenstuff that was a welcome addition to carrots. When we left they loaded us down with all kinds of provisions quite out of proportion to anything that I had been able to do for them.

We had imagined that once we got to Musgrave we should be completely isolated, but during the early autumn ships came into the cove and people came for the week-ends. One Sunday we walked down through the woods to the Mitchells whose house overlooked the Sansum Narrows for a "whisky-drinking and hymn-singing party". The house was robustly and expensively simple, and as the Mitchells only lived there for the three summer months the gloomy darkness which enveloped it during the winter did not affect them. Although most of the party came from Chicago they sang hymns with some of the fervour of frontiersmen, holding their tall glasses full of "whisky-on-the-rocks" and downing them like men. It was like watching the drinking scene in *The Beggar's Opera* become suddenly and sternly Calvinist.

In November the rain started. It rained every day for six weeks punctuated by occasional gales, and it rained all day and all night for a good deal of that time. The bed of the stream became a babbling brook and grew into a foaming torrent. It rose to within a few inches of the bridge and a large section of the path lay under water. The dark pines dripped and dripped.

Before Christmas Clio came back from boarding school with a school friend. Clio was nearly thirteen now and was five foot ten-and-a-half inches tall. She was very slender with the manner of a frisky colt. It was a busy time for presents *had* to be made on the spot, and when I came home in the evening I would find people bent over the workroom benches, others crawling about the floor cutting out designs for penguins, cows or boats. On Christmas Eve Koos and Corrie, with Bertie their kaishond, two yachtsmen who had come into the cove, and all of us from Conspic. Ho. scrambled into the truck with Minnie the goat and Pooh-Bah the Canary Island dog and rumbled down past the cove and up eight hundred feet to the Post Office where Roy lived with his people, and to the various log-cabins of his uncles, all of whom were called Smith. Accompanied by Koos on his accordion we sang both lustily and loud (if not always in tune) all the Christmas carols we could remember. We sang them to each other on the way back, as the truck swayed from side to side and the trees flickered in the glow of the lantern that Clio held on high.

Our last visitors before the winter clamped down were the Sykeses. Vivie and Raith ran a chicken-farm; that is they fattened birds with concentrated feeding, and as long as the birds didn't get some fatal disease during the six weeks that this process took they sold them at a profit. They were considerably younger than either the Smeetons or ourselves and Raith was almost as tall as Miles and considerably broader. They joined in our entertainments with the same abandon as they rounded up a thousand chickens in a night, and I can see Raith now, dressed in a frock made out of two sugar bags, holding Anne, wrapped in a blanket and screaming lustily with tears streaming from her eyes. By his side stood B. the perfect picture of an embarrassed husband, in Miles's only pin-stripe suit, the trousers turned up to the knees, while Miles, looking benignly over his spectacles and dressed in impromptu cassock and surplice, baptized her with rum. I can even remember the word, of two syllables : Churchill.

We loved guests at Conspic. Ho. They were bound to be the right sort, for the wrong would never have stayed. The best

bits of Molly (who had been shot and put in the deep freeze)
came out, and coffee was allowed after dinner. As we stood on
the Government wharf to see the Sykeses off, Vivie kissed Anne,
and said, laughing, "Now, don't forget. Call me and say
'Guests' and those food parcels will be right along."

The curtain rang down on Act 1.

A howling south-easterly gale roared round the house, and
the temperature dropped like a stone. Snow drove over the
tops of the trees and piled against the barn and the sheds in
deep drifts. The wind dropped, and now the flakes fell softly
and relentlessly. In peaked cap and oily, with the collar turned
up and wearing my sea-boots, I took my can of milk and
trudged down the path. From behind me B. flung open the
kitchen window.

"You look like the Retreat from Moscow," she shouted glee-
fully.

The pram was half full of snow and *Moonraker* seemed
buried. I went below and lit the wood stove which the Smeetons had lent us for our stay in B.C. and soon *Moonraker* and I
were a lot warmer than Conspic. Ho. That evening, when
Anne and I walked up through this strange white world,
there was no light shining from Koos's cottage. The power had
gone. And when we got to the house, so had the water.

Miles and B. were bubbling. Crisis! The very spice of life.
No stove, no baths, melted snow in a bucket to drink, and a
good chance that a year's food would go bad in the deep
freeze before the electricity came back. Miles came back from
milking Folly with a broad grin on his face.

"Ha! No logs! All hands tomorrow, Peter."

While Miles, Roy and Koos went off into the woods to look
for frozen sections of pipe, B. and I sawed logs all morning,
and Anne wheeled them in. In the afternoon we took the long
double-ended saw and attacked a tree that had fallen some
months ago. By the time we had made two cuts through that
trunk it appeared to be twelve feet thick, but B. went calmly
on, so I had to, too. I had always felt that Anne was the only
woman I should ever want to sail with on a long sea passage,
but now I would have added another.

Autumn, Musgrave Cove: *Moonraker* and *Tzu Hang*

When it became too dark to see, we stopped, but by then a goodly pile had been stacked under the roof of the veranda, and after they had had time to dry out (if they ever did) we should have something to keep us warm. Back at the house the water was on, and dinner was cooking away on *Tzu Hang's* old Taylor paraffin stove. Conspic. Ho. was under way.

It took ten days and three hours for the deep freeze to rise to melting point and it took ten men ten days and four hours to reach and repair the electric cables that had been twisted and torn by falling trees in the five miles of forest between here and Burgoyne Bay!

For six weeks it snowed and rained and froze and thawed, but never again with the ferocity of that first fall. It was weather for wolves and bears, but wolves kept to the remoter valleys on Vancouver Island, and bears had never been seen on the island, although an occasional cougar swam the Sansum Narrows and plagued the farms. More than once I heard the hoot of an Arctic owl, big enough, Miles said, to carry off a chicken. In the middle of February the sheep started to lamb, and Anne helped to look for lost lambs and to transfer those whose mothers didn't want them to others whose lambs had been lost. Rocky the ram, four-square and with contemplative eyes, seemed enormously proud of his large family. Anne used to take him an apple-core, but if she forgot to keep her eyes on his he'd be waiting to catch her off-balance, and once down she came, much to Rocky's content and Anne's discomfort. It never happened again!

Minnie the goat broke into Folly's bin of oats and ate so much she nearly died, and now B. and Miles couldn't make up their minds whether Folly wanted a bull. Miles was all for taking her to Ganges by sea and B. was for crossing the hill. The snow had almost left Musgrave but at a thousand feet it might still be several feet deep. The glass was tumbling down, and rain was on its way when at last Folly was coaxed into the truck.

Of their adventures Anne wrote in doggerel and Miles illustrated it for Clio.

7

Where the village doctor comes by plane: Desolation Sound, B.C.

We ran into snow that was two feet deep
And trees that had fallen and lay in a heap.
With the winch on the truck we moved them away,
But it took us, you know, the best of the day;
And when to the foot of the hill we came,
We thought some giant had been playing a game,
The trees like Spillikins lay on the ground,
As high as a house and all in a mound,
The road was blocked for half a mile
"Now this," they said, "will take a while."

They'd had no lunch, and they'd had no tea
The trip had been "ill conceived by B."
Miles took his axe and started to hack,
He disregarded the pain in his back,
Into a culvert he staggered and stumbled,
"How unconsidered!" B. thought he mumbled.
After a night tied up to a tree
Alone, deserted by Miles and by B.,
Folly just felt it was meant as a hoax
When B. brought food in a pail to coax.
She stood and shivered and turned away,
"I won't eat oats nor even hay."
I really think she was hurt to the core
"I simply cannot," she said, "stand more,
If this is what cows must do to be mated,
I think that love is over-rated."

Looking back on those lengthening days of late winter the
memory that will stay with me longest is coming down in the
morning before the sun was up and gazing through the drawing-room windows at the land and water that lay spread before
my eyes. Not a thing, I thought, could have changed in a
thousand years except for growth and decay under the hand of
nature; a scene devoid of colour, the grey sky blending with
the distant snows, the dark headland across the straight . . .
all shades from black to white. But this very lack of colour
gave the place a mantle that enhanced its immensity and emphasized the loneliness.

About the middle of March the sun came out and the world

seemed to burst into life. The trees threw off the last traces of snow, lambs cavorted, hens laid, ducks mated, and Minnie forced an entrance in the middle of the night covering the house in dottles. But, as Miles remarked, "Thank goodness, goats are constipated."

There was work at the house and work on the ship. And then one day Roy took all our sails down to the cove in his truck, and I felt the threads of Musgrave begin to stretch and break.

Miles looked round at the evidence of our departure. "We're not coming to see you off," he said. "You're not guests. If we miss you when you come south, we'll see you in England. Good luck!"

And so with a couple of kit-bags slung over our shoulders we walked down the path to where *Moonraker* was lying waiting for us in the cove and I don't believe we exchanged one word until we came aboard.

The other day while I was writing this account a letter came from the Smeetons from Australia. It was from B. and showed a photograph of their Siamese cat sitting on *Tzu Hang's* rail with that watchful look that I have seen in B. herself, wishing us a Happy New Year, and with a brief note saying she would see us in August of this year.

It was as laconic a way as I know of telling us they were bound round Cape Horn from Melbourne, for by no other route could *Tzu Hang* reach England at that time. We had, of course, received a hint of this because, once you have sailed the seven seas, or some of them, you become a member of a "bush telegraph" that is both swift and accurate. We knew that they had a third hand aboard, and a good sailorman at that, and for this we were frankly grateful. The Smeetons, as you may have gathered, are man-sized people, but Cape Horn has a distinctly evil reputation and I for one will be glad when we hear that they have safely weathered it.

CHAPTER THIRTEEN

TO THE QUEEN CHARLOTTE ISLANDS

OUR first sail of the season was a short one of only sixteen miles, but it was a foretaste of what it might be like in the spring. We left the cove with the topsail up, pulled down one and then two reefs and contemplated a third, while squalls of the violence of a gale came tearing off the mountains, driving before them a mist like a plume of smoke. Only the fact that we were sailing in sheltered water prevented us from being hove-to. The spray had the quality of ice, sleet drove against our sodden faces, and we arrived within the shelter of Canoe Cove feeling as if we had done a hard day's work.

The Scott-Moncrieffs came over from Victoria to fetch us. Ronnie Scott-Moncrieff was slightly shorter than I was and when he smiled his whole face wrinkled as if he really meant it. To see him dancing an eightsome reel in the kilt and tartan of his clan reminded me irresistibly of a Scottish chieftain who would defend his castle to the last man and let the enemy in only over his dead body. Lois, his wife, cannot really be described as being passionately fond of boats or the sea, and it would be hard to imagine a worse introduction than hers to *Moonraker*. She had come down with Ronnie on the second morning after our arrival in B.C. Christopher and I, emerging from the engine-room were covered in oil and grease; bits of magneto, valves and spanners lay on the cabin floor, and Ronnie had to sit on the table. But, leading the life we do, it seemed outrageously inhospitable not to ask anyone aboard just because there was no room for them. My wild appearance and the marks of dirt where I had rubbed my nose or an ear may have given me an intimidating appearance, but whatever the cause Lois stepped meekly aboard and sat down on the last inch of settee available. I myself was fascinated (I was leaning on the engine-room doors behind her), for every time I closed my eyes I could hear Marjorie Fielding in *Quiet Week-End*.

The Scott-Moncrieffs' house overlooks Trial Island, and from the drawing-room windows mountains and water vie with each other, so that it is difficult to keep your eyes for long on either. To me it is a more beautiful view than Robert Louis Stevenson's from Black Point in Hiva Oa. The house is so near the water's edge that part of it is bolted down on to a rock, and on a still, misty day the beat of a tanker's diesels coming up the Juan de Fuca Strait is communicated to you as if you were in the cabin of your ship.

It is an open, friendly house and there was much coming and going, for two of their children were still at day schools in Victoria. It became a second home to us.

For our summer cruise we might have been tempted to do nothing more than sail from cove to bay, from one fiord to the next, for it is a curious thing that where inside waters are available the sea takes on a more sinister reputation than it does when you must either face it or give up sailing. Few yachtsmen go to sea in Holland, and during our year's stay in B.C. we met only two that had sailed round Vancouver Island. We received no encouragement to go north from any of our friends except Dave Rogers.

We had first met Dave at Honolulu as a member of the crew of *Dragoon*, from whom we had failed to win a bottle of whisky. He had been a chartered accountant in Vancouver City, had tired of an office life and had bought a fish-boat. For several years he had fished the waters between the Hecate Strait and Cape Flattery, and if he hadn't lost his ship by fire he might well have been there now.

Dave began talking almost at once about the Queen Charlotte Islands, which lie a hundred and twenty miles north-north-west of Vancouver and stretch for two hundred miles north-west of that. He spoke of a place called Two Mountain Bay in Tasu Sound on the West Coast in a slightly lower key, telling us he had weathered the worst sou'-easter he had ever known tied up to half a dozen trees. He compared it to the country round the Magellan Straits and declared there was a saying in these parts that "Men sail the seven seas *and* the Hecate Strait". It seemed a pity now that we were so near not

to go and have a look at it, and when Ronnie said he would
come with us we based our adventure on the Queen Charlotte
Islands. Now the north coast of the Charlottes is only thirty
miles from the shores of Alaska. Although no one in B.C.
thinks anything of going there (by the Inside Passage) those
in England might think of Eskimos and Polar Bears. So Ketchikan was added to our list.

One evening Dave and Willi, his wife, came up to the Scott-
Moncrieffs and four heads were bent in earnest concentration over a mass of charts and sailing directions. Chairs and
sofas had been pushed away and Lois and Willi held a watching brief. It was a little hard on Lois, I thought, that Dave had
to develop some sort of conscience that very night about sending us up to those bleak and inhospitable shores.

He told us, as others had, that we shouldn't leave the inland waters until the beginning of June, that sou'-easters in the
Hecate Strait were dangerous not only by reason of the shallow
waters, the unpredictable currents and the unlit dangers, but
also the heavy rain, which invariably accompanies these storms
and cuts visibility to a mile. He gave instances of strandings
and shipwrecks, of fishermen who had lost their lives off Rose
Spit. Ronnie was as enthralled as we were, but it might, I
thought, be a different matter for his wife to listen to what
must sound like the measured tread of a pavane with death.
Lois is a quiet person. I watched her sitting there without a
movement of her hands, a little smile playing round her mouth
at some of Dave's more dramatic moments. Finally she
spoke:

"Mr Rogers, surely in summer the weather is not as bad as
all that?"

"You never know," answered Dave. "The worst gale I was
out in was in August. It blew the best part of a hundred knots
and I remember a large American boat, not fifty yards away,
trying to make for shelter. One moment she was there and the
next she'd gone, without a trace."

Lois laughed a little uncertainly. "Put it this way," she said.
"If Peter and Anne asked you to go on *Moonraker*, would you go
to the west coast of the Charlottes with them?"

"Of course. It's only that I want Peter to know what sort of place he's going to."

Anne and I took *Moonraker* up the Gulf of Georgia, in and out of islands, though the Porlier Pass where the pram half filled in the tide rips, sailed across the Georgia Strait (the width of the Straits of Dover) with a topsail breeze and came in the evening into Burrard Inlet, where the wind dropped. I towed our old ship into Star Boat Cove just to the east of Point Atkinson. The lights came out in tall buildings and were reflected in the glassy waters of the inlet, and the last rays of the sun glowed on the snows of the higher peaks that surround Vancouver to the north and east. The roar of a great city came to our ears blurred by the blessed distance of the five miles that lay between it and us.

I have often wondered what the place looks like from the air. It is built, of course, in squares and blocks like all North American cities but it may easily seem more compact than it appears from the ground. We were told that the first baby ever to be registered within the city precincts was still alive; and now 700,000 people live here.

Bob Harlow lives, like a hawk in its eyrie, at the very top of the Vancouver Hotel and directs the talks side of the C.B.U. He speaks very rapidly, and he had made it quite plain (on our first visit) that he was interested neither in boats nor in the people who sailed them.

"But write a few scripts if you like," he said, "and I'll look at them."

It was to record these and to spend some time with friends in the city that we were now here. One day I had a telephone message from Bob saying that he wanted to come down and see us. He sat in the cabin, looking a little lost carrying an umbrella and in his town clothes. I gave him a drink.

"I don't know what you folks have done to me," he said, "but I've bought a boat."

On a golden day in May Ronnie and Lois picked us up and drove us along the Fraser Valley, up the Fraser Canyon to Ashcroft and Kamloops, to the Selkirks and then down the Okenagen Valley. We spent the nights in log cabins and slept to the sound of rushing mountain streams or to the stillness of a lake.

Ronnie took things quietly, driving a hundred and fifty miles a day, and the only disappointment was that the road to the Rockies was still blocked by snow. One of the great disadvantages in travelling in your own boat is that there is so rarely a chance to know more than the watery edge of the country in which you find yourself, but this expedition gave us at least an idea of what B.C. was like behind the great barrier of the Coastal Range. We thought it wonderful.

Back on the ship we made ready for Dave and Willi to join us for the first week of our trip towards the north. This first part of our voyage lay through broad stretches of water, past clusters of islands, across the mouths of deep fiords; good sailing if only there had been enough wind. He took us into coves, gorges and sounds that we might never have discovered for ourselves.

At one settlement, Whaletown, where there was a float to which you could tie up, a store with a deep-freeze and any provisions you liked to buy, we walked up the road to find a little church built very simply of wood, painted white and shining in the afternoon sun. It had been built as a memorial to John Ansel who had been the first man to found a mission on this lonely coast which, for weeks at a time, is cut off in the winter. He spent most of his life among the islands and on the west coast of Vancouver Island using his own ship as headquarters until missions could be established ashore. After he retired (he must have been well over seventy) he sailed his vessel, a gaff-rigged ketch rather like a small Brixham trawler, down to Panama with the help of two girls. From there they set off to Jamaica and had a rough passage, we heard, and then, just as they sighted the island Father Ansel had a stroke. It must have been a hard decision to make, but those girls thought it would take longer to reach the island, some fifty or sixty miles to windward, than to run back the four hundred miles to Colon. With the current against them, I'm sure they were right, and John Ansel was still alive when they sailed in between the breakwaters.

Every ship that sails north inside Vancouver Island must pass through either the Seymour Narrows or the Yaculta Rapids. The tide runs through the Narrows up to seventeen knots although the more usual rate is twelve to fourteen. In the middle of the narrowest part lies the Ripple Rock over which there is nine feet of water at low water springs. At various times people have tried to blow it up to reduce the tremendous eddies that it causes, and once a barge sixty feet long with eight men aboard was moored to the rock. In the heavy overfalls of a particularly strong flood the barge capsized and all eight men were drowned. When we heard this story we thought we'd try the Yaculta Rapids but, unfortunately, we met a man who had been through the Yaculta Rapids. His vessel was a Tahiti ketch and however much you may dislike this type of craft she is at least buoyant. Coming through on the flood he had the unusual experience of watching his stern disappear in a whirlpool. It came up again, of course, but he had never felt quite the same person since.

We chose the Seymour Narrows. The tides are worked out to the nearest minute with the rates of the stream for every hour. Slack water lasts for twelve minutes. With Ted Rose, a doctor friend of Ronnie's who had come (he said) to see how to sail in these waters without an engine, we left Campbell River, six miles to the south, at what we thought was the right time. The wind was light ahead, and as soon as I felt the force of the stream I knew we should arrive far too early. There seemed only one thing to do; we swung the ship round till she faced the way she had come, set the spinnaker, and continued towards the narrows backwards at about the pace we wanted. The wind died away. Overshadowed by high, pine-covered hills black under a lowering sky the dominant note was of gloom, a gloom that was deepened on our ship by one of our engine's two cylinders taking a day off. With lifeless sails we were drifting through the water when a ten-thousand-ton steamer that had been waiting at anchor got under way. Right between Ripple Rock and the mainland we were caught in the grip of an eddy and swept across her bows. I saw Anne's white face looking up at the advancing bows and I knew she knew that that steamer had to keep straight on no matter what lay in her path.

"Fools rush in . . ." I muttered, when a smart breeze swept down a valley and filled our sails. In a moment the steamer was past, a group of men standing on her bridge, as if turned to stone, looking down upon us.*

There were now ten minutes to go before the tide was due to turn. The breeze faltered. With our eyes on the clock we crawled like an injured snail towards Brown's Bay and on the tenth minute (this is God's truth) we slipped into the quiet water of that cove. Ted broke the silence as we stood watching the flood sweeping down Discovery Passage.

"You two do take your pleasures in a most peculiar way," he said, mopping his brow, and I thought I heard Anne murmur, "With one hand in God's pocket and very tightly clenched."

Up the interminable Johnstone Strait, as long as that of Juan de Fuca, we beat and beat against a fresh west wind, while high mountains gave place to lower ones, and the pine trees grew shorter, until one morning we were shot out into the broad expanse of Queen Charlotte Sound. Sea and sky were a uniform grey with islands like humps on camel's backs, indescribably lonely and forbidding. For the first time the ship stirred to the ocean swell and the glass fell, slowly and steadily.

Opposite the northern end of Vancouver Island the mainland is outflanked by rocks and reefs, by sounds and inlets, while to the north-west islands large and small give protection to deep channels that wind towards Alaska. Outside these islands the coast is fringed by groups of islets, passages marked "unexamined" and the whole coast is wide open to the Pacific Ocean.

It was to explore this coast that we set out with Ronnie Scott-Moncrieff who flew up (there is no road north of Campbell River) to take Ted's place at Port Hardy. Our first day

---

* In case anyone should be deterred by our experiences it is only fair to add that navigation is safe enough through the Seymour Narrows if carried out within an hour either side of slack water *provided* that the vessel is equipped with an adequate engine. Without this it is a hazardous proceeding.

ended at Finn Bay at the mouth of Rivers Inlet. The weather had behaved much as Dave had said it might, the bright morning giving way to a threatening sky, a rising wind and squalls of rain which blotted out the landmarks in a most disconcerting way. It was dusk by the time we reached shelter and shook out the reefs, and so narrow was the entrance to Finn Bay that we nearly missed it—a tiny gap in a forest of pines through which we half drifted towards a cluster of lights on the starboard hand. This turned out to be a fish camp; a scow moored to the bank with chains. There was a store, ice for keeping fish (hardly necessary, we felt), two tanks of "gas" and half a dozen fish-boats.

Unseen voices asked us where we'd come from and who we were and when we'd told them we'd crossed Queen Charlotte Sound one of them said, "Didn't you listen to the forecast? It's blowing fifty knots."

Looking back on the short time we spent on that bit of coast I can't remember anything I have enjoyed more. "Local knowledge is essential," is how the *Pilot* would describe some of the places we poked our noses into, and I must admit there were times when a little would have come in handy. A snap decision of mine to take the Kwakshua Channel (marked "unexamined") nearly landed us in trouble, but it was cool and quiet as a cave when we turned to starboard down a narrow gully that cuts Hecate Island in half, passed between two islets and out into Hakai Pass.

The great Pacific rollers came tramping in on the wings of a fresh breeze, columns of spray like depth charges rose in all directions and we looked in vain for an expected light tower.* For a moment I could see no way out. The sea, however, was breaking on anything we were likely to hit, and by a process of elimination and a determined will to survive we mastered the intricacies of this unpleasant situation and shaped a course to clear all visible dangers.

Old *Moonie* went like a train, breasting the seas with that surprising power that she packs into her short little body, and I found myself falling in love with her all over again. The

* It had been destroyed in the recent winter gales.

fresh wind, the big sea, the brassy glare of the sun as it sank towards the west gave that touch of anxiety which makes it so much more fun (and the more advisable) to find an anchorage for the night.

We were bound for Spider Anchorage, where several narrow entrances led to a landlocked lagoon. In the circumstances only one was possible. I identified Spider Island, the key to the spider's web, and we came tearing in with seas breaking on either side and it was at that moment that Anne cast doubt into my mind. There were no marks or lights or buoys, of course, and one islet looks very like another. Point and counter point flew across the deck till Anne herself solved the problem by climbing up to the crosstrees and seeing in front of her, through a passage in a wall of rock, the lagoon itself. I relaxed, but Ronnie was not used to this.

"You're like a couple of children," he muttered. "Why can't you make up your minds and stick to it?"

Why not, indeed; but suppose I had been wrong?

In time we acquired some sort of local knowledge ourselves. A fisherman came aboard at Spider bringing a present of a salmon.

"You folks should visit Codfish Camp," he said, "they'd sure be glad to see you." He put a horny hand on a dozen islands (so small a scale are the only charts available): "The camp's in there. You want to look out for a rock off that point and there's a shoal in here . . . turn in and you'll find the scow moored there."

They were certainly pleased to see us. At every camp there would be some story of the life along the coast; we were told of the seiner which, a hundred miles off-shore, dropped her propeller into the drink. Her skipper hewed down the bulkheads, made two paddle-wheels of them, rigged his mast athwartship and drove the paddles with his winch engine. By the time they made port the pole had eaten right through his bulwarks and through half the deck as well. There wasn't a smear of grease or butter left on that ship!

And then there was the ship that steered herself. . . . We heard that one from Jim, the storekeeper at Codfish. Jim and his brother left Vancouver City bound for Selwyn Inlet on the Charlottes in their salmon troller. The weather was thick all the way up and when they got into the Hecate Strait it was so thick that you couldn't see the bow from the wheelhouse. They had been doing watch and watch for two days and a night and Jim said he was pretty tired as he took over at midnight. About six that morning, just as it was getting light but just as thick as ever, Jim peered into the compass bowl in a dazed sort of a way and suddenly realized he'd been standing there for his whole watch, sound asleep! In something near a panic, he called his brother. He said, "Look, Ed, I've been asleep the whole of my blessed watch."

"No, you wasn't," replied his brother, " 'cos I came up about two hours ago and you talked to me. You was on course too."

Jim scratched his head, "Darn that," he said, "I know I been asleep. We may have been waltzin' about all over the blinkin' Strait."

And at that moment the curtain lifted a trifle and there they were steaming up Selwyn Inlet!

We ourselves were bound there a few days later from Camano Sound, ninety miles across the Hecate Strait.

I went on watch at four in the morning. We should, I thought, be approaching Selwyn Inlet. A fine drizzle drove through the air on a rising southerly wind, the ceiling was down to a hundred feet, and visibility was under a mile. Ronnie, blue with cold, was at the helm. I fussed over the chart. There should be an off-lying island, the only distinctive one on the coast. Suddenly Ronnie's shout:

"Land," he cried, "above us!"

And out of the mist, like the long edge of a saw, cut Reef Island, dead ahead.

CHAPTER FOURTEEN

THROUGH THE HECATE STRAIT TO ALASKA

FROM the chart the Queen Charlotte Islands look like a great kite, flown on a hundred and twenty miles of string from the top of Vancouver Island. When I first bought a general chart I thought they'd made a mistake and given me a map, so empty of figures were the sounds and fiords that penetrate their rugged coastline. Although there are reputed to be two hundred islands in all, there are two main ones, Graham in the North and Moresby in the South. Our first introduction to them, Selwyn Inlet on Moresby, was typical. Dark pines clung to almost impossible slopes which rose into mist and cloud. Cold, bleak and wet.

And yet to me, as we sailed into this deep fiord, it was more exciting than anything I had seen before. It was the remoteness, the savagery of the place, a thing I cannot do justice to in words. There should by rights have been nothing there at all, so that it came as something of an anti-climax to turn a corner and find, facing us, a logging camp and people.

The camp consisted of a long green building with an outhouse for the plant, which made the electricity. The bunkhouse, for that was the name they gave to their living quarters, was kept scrupulously clean, and the long deal tables were laid for supper; clean white plates, white cups, tablecloths and large white notices which read, "Please after your meal put your silverware into the pail. Thank you."

We met the High Rigger, paid at twenty dollars a day, whose job it was to rig the "skyline", a mast with pulleys, blocks and cables for shifting trees from where they were cut down to the "coal deck"; the "Fallers" who are paid by piece work. "They either get rich or get killed" we were told and we gathered the odds were little better than even. The loggers were a young, tough crowd, but work kept them out of mischief, and no drink was allowed in the camp. The Superintendent was new. He had been sent out to replace one who had not been able to keep harmony, for the men's isolation is complete: no roads, no outside entertainments, no women (except for a single wife who looked as if she found her position to be not altogether without strain), mail once a week by bush plane, casualties evacuated by seaplane.

These islands were, and are, inhabited by Haida Indians, a tribe lighter in colour than the coastal Indians and, except for their more oriental eyes, remarkably like the Polynesians. Some were tall and of fine physique and they had had the reputation of being the fiercest warriors along a thousand miles of coast. Legend has it that they came across the Bering Strait while it was still land and settled in the Queen Charlotte Islands. Constant raids on the mainland kept them free from too much in-breeding and preserved the race.

A little to the north of Selwyn Inlet lies the deserted village of Skedans. We arrived off the peninsula on which the village was built in the early evening. It was open to the Hecate Strait and not a place that a prudent mariner chooses to spend the night in, but the glass was high and what breeze there was came off the land.

What a perfect place to defend! To landward a steep and rocky bluff, to seaward a small hill that had been fortified and could be defended to the last man. On each side of the peninsula was a beach, so that the returning warriors could use either side according to the wind and I could imagine the victorious fleet sailing in after carrying the war into the enemy's country as far south as Discovery Island in Vancouver harbour four hundred miles away, whose name in Indian days, after the Haidas had been there, was Dead Man's Island.

Totem poles, magnificently carved, but bare of paint and rotting fast, stood among the trees and the long grass, some straight, others at a drunken angle. The archway of a meeting house was entwined by undergrowth; and we found, in what must have been the tribal burial ground, the bleached skulls and bones of children. Sixty years ago seven thousand Haidas lived in the valleys near Skedans when, with the suddenness of the plague, smallpox wiped out all but two hundred. No Haida has ever spend a night there since.

It was getting dark when Anne almost stepped on a day-old fawn. Its body was beautifully marked with spots and stripes of white against its warm brown coat. Her hand went down.

Ronnie said, quickly, "Don't touch it. If you do the mother will never come back. She's probably watching you."

Twenty miles north of Skedans Point lies Sand Spit and the entrance to Skidegate Inlet. It is, from a pilot's point of view, a remarkable place, for right across the entrance to the Inlet and for seven miles to the north runs a sand bar too shallow to cross with six-foot draught at low water. The wind had freshened and we were making for Dead Tree Point, sounding furiously with the lead while the ship buried her lee rail under a press of canvas. There was, we found, more water than the chart marked, and we were soon easing sheets for the run up the inlet. Broad and well protected by the bar, dotted with islands and fair of face, this fiord bends to starboard, and round the corner we were confronted with the snows of the Slatechuck Mountain and the buildings of Queen Charlotte City, all twenty-four houses of it, which with a church, three stores and a hospital, go to make this northern metropolis. We entered the tiny harbour under sail, clawed down the canvas, let the halyards run and came alongside the float. A little group of people had gathered to take our lines, and a thin, gaunt man with blue eyes and a brogue, whom men called Paddy, leaned over our bulwarks and said in a hoarse whisper, "Sure, an' you're the first boat to sail in here from England in a hundred years."

We stayed for three days. We had been warned that you must never ask anyone in Queen Charlotte City why he lived there.

"There is always some very good reason," we were told, "but not one they like to talk about."

They took us over the hospital, the little church, the school, (for Haidas and whites) where I showed some coloured slides of the South Sea Islands. They fed us, they washed our clothes and offered us baths. No community ever did more to give strangers a free run of their little town.

Our last day we spent at the Haida village three miles down the Inlet. The houses were a little bare of paint, and inside they

The abandoned village of Skedans

A wild and savage land: the Queen Charlotte Islands

Ronnie would be in Victoria tonight

were as empty of anything but the essentials as a Tahitian's hut, and just as clean. We talked to fishermen, one of whom had lost his big seiner off Rose Spit a month or two ago, and to the Old Men of the Tribe who spend their time making models of totem poles in the Slatechuck stone which, when polished, resembles ebony. One man had a face like our pilot who had so hazardously taken us out of the lagoon at Takaroa. He was working on a medallion on which he had carved a vigorous-looking raven in relief. While he worked away with a minute chisel he started to tell us the story of the Raven and the Moon:

Long, long ago a raven killed the child of the owner of the moon, climbed into his skin, cried until the parents gave him the moon to play with, and then, when no one was looking, slipped out of the baby's skin and flew up through the smoke hole with the moon tucked under his wing. He flew to Nass River where he came upon some Oolaken fishermen who refused him fish unless he gave them light. Much to their delight he pulled out the moon and, tearing bits off with his powerful beak, he threw the pieces into the sky to make the stars, the sun and the moon. Although it was a little difficult to understand this rambling tale (which I have considerably shortened) it does explain why, on their totem poles, the raven is displayed in such a prominent position.

That evening we sailed across the sound to Alliford bay, making fast to a disused R.C.A.F. buoy. There wasn't a breath of wind and the bay was as still as a pond. I told Anne and Ronnie to make fast with an old coir rope. We turned in.

I was dimly aware of a shattering noise going on all too close to my ear. It was no human sound, nor had it anything to do with the sea. I opened my eyes. Halfway between a squawk and a screech, that's what it was. I turned out of our warm bunk to see a raven striding round the bulwarks. But when he saw me, instead of flying away, his eyes glowed with fury, he flapped his wings and intensified the squawking. I went up on deck, and with one last baleful look he flew away. I looked ahead. *Moonie*, under bare poles, was sailing herself towards the rockstrewn entrance to the bay.

8

By mid-day the old ship, under main, topsail and spinnaker, was out in the Hecate Strait. At its southern end it is a hundred miles across, a width it maintains for two hundred miles until the northern end is reached. Here the navigable width is limited by the overfalls off Rose Spit and the reefs off the B.C. coast to less than twenty miles. As it trends to the north-north-west the bottom shelves from fifty fathoms to nine. The south-easters, for which it is notorious, as Dave had said, funnel up the narrowing seaway with increasing strength and fury.

On this lovely day, with a steady glass and an off-shore wind, I went below without a care in the world. I think it was the feeling of strain that woke me a bare two hours later, and never have I seen weather change in so short a time or in so sinister a manner. A pall of light brown cloud covered the entire sky, and small wet cotton-wool clouds hung in the mountain valleys. To port the low coastline of Graham Island was all too close. By five o'clock we had two reefs in the main-sail, by six, three; by seven, four. We hove her to.

Wet, cold and anxious, I took a last look round and followed the others below. From time to time I cast a glance at Ronnie, for this was his first real gale, but from the quiet way he was chopping sticks with our blunt axe and gathering brickettes and bark for the fire it worried him as little as it would have done a fish.

The Hecate Strait was living up to its reputation: the wind howling out of the sou'-east, the smoking sea, steep and ugly as if it was scooping the very mud off the bottom, the ship blinded by the fury of the elements. Sail had to come off. With in-finite care, for our lives depended upon it, we got the mainsail down, lashing gaff and boom to gallows. Turning, we ran under bare poles towards the Dixon Entrance. She was running too fast. I think Anne and I must have thought of the warps at the same moment, for without a word I saw her and Ronnie paying out the two thirty-fathom warps astern and after that I knew that if I could keep the vessel off the rocks she would still be afloat in the morning.

So successful had Ronnie been with the fire that the whole stove glowed. Between our one-hour watches (so bitterly cold was it on deck that we could stand no more) I sat over it warming my frozen hands. I remembered a story of Conrad's, it may have been his own, of how, as mate, he went up for his master's ticket. He was asked what he would do if his ship was driving down on the North German coast and as fast as he tried to extricate his hapless vessel, the examiner removed the means by which he attempted to do so.

At last he said, "I'm sorry, sir, but there's nothing more that I can do."

"Dammit, man," cried the examiner, "can't you pray?"

Soon after dawn I must have dozed for a few minutes. Anne was asleep in her bunk in her oily and sea-boots, and I heard Ronnie's shout.

I looked out on that waste of water. It was still blowing hard, but the rain had stopped and three islands to starboard gave us our position. The shores of Alaska were dimly visible ahead.

The glass, which had fallen rather more than half an inch, still fell, and as we entered Clarence Strait heavy squalls fell upon us. In thirty hours, I see from my log, we reefed and un-reefed that main eleven times. We tore up Nicholls Passage. Black mountains whose tops were white with fresh snow frowned down upon us, as if unwilling to welcome such an insignificant intruder to so wild a land. We shot into the Tongass Narrows—it was the 14th of June.

The neat, white little town of Ketchikan appeared ahead, a kindly fish-boat told us where to berth. We ran into the small boat harbour and let everything go with a run, only to haul all up again as the ship was gripped in a strong current that threatened to throw her out. It took us thirty minutes to sail thirty yards, and by that time we were being cheered from the bank like a football team.

We were, as you can imagine, pretty tired. The Customs came to clear us. They asked us many questions about the voyage and then they left. As they walked up the float I heard one of them say:

"Two of those guys are M.D.s. You'da' thought they'da' had more sense!"

CHAPTER FIFTEEN

KETCHIKAN TO TWO MOUNTAIN BAY

RAIN. Drizzle or downpour from racing clouds and a pall over-hanging the mountains, people striding from street to street taking as much notice of the wet as an African does of the sun, a river running past Indian huts built on stilts against the spring floods, a harbour full of fish-boats, for they said this was the worst spring they could remember. And then, one morning, sun shining from a pale blue sky. The whole face of the little town changed. The vivid greens of the hemlock, the dazzling snows that seemed to come right down almost to the town itself, the white buildings washed by the rains and the wooden roads supported by long piles like trellis-work, scrubbed and weathered to a pale grey.

Although Ketchikan is no longer a frontier town it has a pioneering air. People are far too busy making money to have time for the pursuits of leisure, but they have one fixed and common purpose, to leave Ketchikan as soon as they are able; the young to go on, the more mellow to go back, if possible to somewhere warmer like Honolulu. All, that is, except the fishermen. But fishermen are like farmers; they grumble but they never quit.

All this abominable weather began to make us feel we might have to beat back to Victoria, so we cut short our stay and on an afternoon of no wind we left under engine (our engine liked Ronnie and had allowed him to coax it into action) bound for Prince Rupert to "clear" for Canada. Our course never took us out of sight of land and we were now well stocked with American charts. That night we put into Hasler Harbour, a misleading name for what is no more than a bay protected from Revillagigedo Channel by an island whose shores seemed to be covered with green sand. I meant to go and have a look at that sand, but a fisherman came chugging in round the other side of the island and her owner held up a salmon.

"This any good to you?" he called.

To which Ronnie promptly answered, "Is it not!" and rowed off to collect the fish and ask our friend to share it.

His name was Jim Gordon, for fourteen years a radio-operator in Pan-American Airways.

"The pay-cheque was good," he said, "but when they grounded me I quit."

He came to the north-west, bought a fish-boat in Seattle and fished the Alaskan waters in the summer. So far he'd been able to keep himself during the winter, run a car and go down Mexico way for a bit of sun. No, he'd never had anyone else aboard and never missed the company that another would have given him. He'd been out for the last two weeks and was returning to Ketchikan with a boat full of fish. But Jim was more than a fisherman, he was a born seaman. In this short time he had acquired a mass of information about coves and holes among the rocks where he had weathered severe storms, and he talked as a man who has spent his life on the coast. He had a voice rather like Raymond Gram Swing to whom we used to listen so intently during the war.

It was still light when he left us, around eleven, but now the cove was quiet. The golden eagles, of which we had seen at least a dozen when we first arrived, had stopped talking to each other, and the clouds had lifted revealing a cold northern sky. It was strangely colourless, for it was almost time for the sun to go to bed.

Our last night in Alaska was spent tucked up in one of Jim's holes behind Cape Fox. The glass was falling, but we were wet, cold and very tired; nor was it prudent to sail these waters at night because of the danger of hitting logs. So we dropped anchor and set the alarm for three o'clock. It needed no alarm to wake me. A fresh east wind blew straight in and one look at the sky and the glass warned us that another sou'-easter was on its way. We beat out and soon we were at it again shortening sail, reef after reef, while endless rain went through our oilskins like water through a sieve. It must be quite a time, I thought, since there had been anything dry aboard. We reached the Metlakatla channel, a short cut to Prince Rupert, but so narrow and winding did it appear on our chart that I should not have had the courage to attempt it had it not been for Jim. It meandered past an Indian village, past sandy bays where for once hills and mountains seemed pushed away. Above all, it was smooth and quiet after the turmoil outside.

Prince Rupert did not look attractive. It is an untidy, top-heavy sort of a place, the skeleton of a businessman's dream of a great city, a future golden gateway to the Orient. Unfortunately the businessman went down with the *Titanic* forty years ago, since when no one has thought Prince Rupert to be worth while. The town is some distance from the dock, and not for a minute, not for a second, did it stop raining.

But there is something I like to remember. We were tied up to the Prince Rupert Yacht and Rowing Club. We had by this time exhausted our supply of "gas" (most of it had gone on priming) so I took our three two-gallon cans to the man who looked after the gas station. I pulled out a five-dollar bill but he firmly shook his head.

"I read in some newspaper you'd sailed from England to Victoria on twelve gallons," he laughed, "I guess I'd like to give you this to get you home."

The west coast of the Queen Charlotte Islands where we were now bound is as wild and rugged, so we had been told, as the Magellan country. Inhabited by bears, eagles and deer but not by man, it is indented by inlets and fiords and visited by fishermen during the summer; and by one other sailorman. He was the sort about whom legends grow up overnight. Some said he was an ex-Royal Navy man, others that his sister owned a great house in Mayfair (and a Rolls-Royce) but the men in the Charlottes knew him for a superb seaman to whom the whole coast from Cape St. James to Dutch Harbour in the Aleutian Islands was an open book. Before I had heard anything about him I came down one morning to Musgrave Cove to find a stranger lying at anchor. She was a gaff cutter with an enormous exhaust pipe coming out of the after end of the cabin and she looked so weathered that she fitted into her bleak surroundings (it was snowing and bitterly cold) as a thrush into a hedge. She had an air about her that dissuaded me from immediately calling on her owner, and by the time I next looked out she had gone.

We saw her only once more, in the spring, running before half a gale of wind down an inside passage. Her owner, bearded, blended with the appearance of his ship and looked as silent and as taciturn as he was in fact reputed to be. We half hoped to see him on this coast where he had made his name.

We slipped out of Brown's Passage on the tail of the last sou'-easter. We crossed the Hecate Strait making for the west coast of the Queen Charlottes. By the afternoon of the following day we were within five miles of Langara Island, off the north-western tip of Graham Island. "So near," Ronnie was to say, "and yet so far away . . ." For within the hour the wind had switched from east to west bringing with it a thin, tenuous mist from the cold Pacific.

The uncertain currents, the light head-wind, the unreliable log, after five hours of beating to and fro all I knew was that I had no idea where I was. And then, just before I handed the ship over to Ronnie the mist lifted to port, and there was a small square of land like a window in a wall, bearing south-east. But what land was it?

Anne, pouring the water from the pressure cooker into a basin on deck, gave it a glance. "Langara Island?" she asked.

"Good Lord," I said. "Perhaps it is."

Although it disappeared almost immediately, the more I thought of it the more determined I became that it must be the west coast of Langara, and I worked out a course for Ronnie that would take him down to Port Louis.

I was not asleep when Ronnie called me. "Peter, come up a moment, will you?"

He said, "I can hear birds twittering, land birds, to star-board."

I looked at him blankly.

"That means there's land to starboard," he explained patiently.

"The nearest land," I muttered, "should be a thousand miles away."

Ronnie's face sharpened. "Can't you hear them?"

"Yes, but one bird is the same as another to me."

And at that moment I heard another sound, one that I knew only too well: breakers. Even then I didn't stumble on what we'd done. We hauled our wind making north of west and still the land, now dimly seen as a darker grey, clung to us like a limpet, and then the mist cleared for a moment and I saw the light in Parry Passage, bearing south. We'd come right down the wrong side of Langara Island.

But I knew where I was now, in a tideless backwater, Nigeria Bay, and there we stayed all night, *Moonraker* lying like a dog at her master's feet; for there wasn't a breath of wind, and it was too deep to anchor.

The sound of a high-speed engine brought me on deck at dawn to see a fish-boat circling round and round us.

Her owner hailed me: "Why don't you come into Henslung Camp?"

"No wind," I shrugged, "and our engine's broken down."

"Aw, there's no fish in the sea this morning," he said. "Throw me a line and I'll tow you in."

The radio and a Prince Rupert newspaper had mentioned our appearance on the coast, and curiosity was rife. The fish-camp (there were really two, one where the men owned their own boats, the other in which the Company owned the boats and hired the men) was the largest we had seen. It was like a little floating town, and there were few things that a seaman might want that could not be had at the store: our petrol pipe was mended within the hour. Some of the men fished alone, others with their wives. There was a girl from Liverpool, a man from Devon, a private secretary to one of the heads of the C.P.R. who preferred the sea to the office, and a chief of the Eagle tribe whose grandfather had owned the last three-masted schooner on the coast. The talk was of fish and boats, of the seiners (like the wicked uncles) who netted fish in the rivers (for this was a camp of trollers) and the paucity of salmon. A halibut was plopped on our deck and out of courtesy Anne saw no alternative to cooking all forty pounds of it on her single Primus!

By the time we were up next morning there wasn't a boat in

the place, so we followed their example and put to sea, a calm, smiling sea and a light following wind and *sun*! At first the coast resembled that of Cornwall, but before we came to Port Louis in the evening sombre snow-clad mountains appeared to the south. Port Louis is supposed to be the one harbour on the west coast that is safe to run for if caught by bad weather, but to us, that evening, it looked inexpressibly gloomy. The fresh wind astern, the clusters of islands in the deep and frowning bay, the sea breaking on reefs, no lights, no marks and two islets that we had to identify, one of two hundred feet and one of one hundred and fifty, made a little more difficult by the taller of the two having recently lost its trees!

At the entrance to the bay in which we hoped to anchor the wind was cut off, and we half drifted, half carried our way into this silent pool whose name was Kialthli Inlet. There was not a sound . . . not a cry of a bird, not a whisper of the sea on a beach, not a stir in the forest. A blood-red sunset bathed the trees in a gory light. It would have been a good place for Miss Greta Garbo.

From here to Tasu Sound is the finest coast, if you like your coasts to look like this, that I have ever seen: high mountains, precipitous ravines, black forests, desolate and forbidding; a coast to make you ponder on the insignificance of man. A fair wind had taken us south-eastwards all day, but in the evening it fell too light for us to make Tasu before nightfall. What a place, I kept telling myself, to be hove to. But the night was short, and by four o'clock we were under way to a freshening onshore breeze and a falling glass. The sea was a bottle green. The wind backed, and it became a race between us and the weather, with the odds increasingly against us.

Grey cliffs, their tops lost in the gathering clouds, fell sheer into the sea, a great wall of rock through which, at two hundred yards from the entrance, no hole could be seen. Clouds swirled down from the heights above, and if they blocked the entrance before we found it we were due for a nice long wait on a cold and angry sea. But we beat 'em! On the next board there was the opening and, like a glimpse of a promised land, we saw the sun still shining on a blue and glittering lake.

"Down topsail," I shouted, as the ship, with the sheets just started, raced for the narrow opening, and as we entered this rocky gorge the clouds came down to the level of the sea and it was like running into a tunnel full of smoke. Squalls from either side, water the colour of ink flecked with white where the wind whipped it round; then we were out on the other side, the sou'-easter still held at mountain level from breaking in.

We spent three days in Tasu Sound. Most of the time it rained and blew, but even a hurricane could not have hurt us in such a sheltered place and the stove burned merrily day and night. We had heard that a trail once led over the mountains from Two Mountain Bay to Selwyn Inlet but we found no tracks except those made by bear and deer. Anne saw a cub run up a tree and was quietly going to talk to it when Ronnie pulled her away. His sharp eyes had seen the mother sitting at the bottom! A trail led us to a waterfall. The pool into which the fall cascaded was brown, for this was cedar water, poisonous to most people, and we had been told that fishermen wrecked on this coast had died of thirst. This we found hard to believe, for all we would have had to have done was to open our mouths and lift them up.

Ronnie took a rifle ashore to shoot deer but he went alone, for Anne and I are not at our best in undergrowth, and as Ronnie so rightly said, "How can I stalk deer with you crashing through the forest like a herd of elephants."

We sailed into Wright's Inlet. This, to our minds, was the finest anchorage of them all. It was a little unfortunate that on that very day the Baby Blake got blocked. Ronnie and I spent the whole afternoon in the fo'c'sle bent double over it but in the end we carried it triumphantly through the cabin and hoisted it on deck. Ronnie said firmly, "I'm going ashore to get a stick to clean the outlet pipe." It occurred to me, after an hour had passed, that he was finding it extremely difficult.

There were now eight days of Ronnie's leave to go. The distance to Victoria was 473 miles and there was time enough, I thought, to visit at least one inlet on the west coast of Vancouver. Ronnie, who has lived on Vancouver Island most of his life, did not share my view. Head winds, moderate to strong, prevailed until we sighted Cape Cook; followed by calms. Fourteen hours here, seventeen hours off Cape Estevan. I saw what Ronnie meant.

We could not land him, as there are no roads across Van-couver Island, no roads, indeed, of any sort until you get down to Bamfield where there is a boat to Alberni. This, then, was the position at noon on July 5. The ship was becalmed off Clayo-quot Sound, and Bamfield lay forty miles to the south-east; Ronnie's leave was up in two days. In the evening a northerly wind sprang up, freshened, and veered to the north-east. That ancient rhyme:

> Last night the sun went pale to bed
> The moon in haloes hid her head

fitted the portents perfectly, and during my watch the glass dropped like a stone. Driving rain, two reefs in the main, fol-lowed by three and then four, a short steep sea—how sick we were of these sou'-easters!

We plunged on, for I was determined to land Ronnie if it was humanly possible. The wind, I argued, was along the coast, I should recognize Cape Beale if I saw it; but what if I could not find it? We stood in for the land. Two hours later, with the tension mounting, minute by minute, I caught through the murk what I took to be a high bluff of land. Wherever that bluff was, it wasn't Cape Beale, and at that moment it really started to blow. We got the ship about at the third attempt, and for half an hour we ran with the sea and wind abeam to make a much-needed offing. It was a most exciting sail, but in the end, as I was afraid it might, a sea swept the ship.

Ronnie, who was for'ard lashing down a coil of rope, jumped for the ratlines, Anne and I were lifted right off the deck, cling-ing to the gallows, and, like the owner of the Tahiti ketch in the Yaculta Rapids, we watched the after end of our ship dis-appear below the sea. The oars were swept from under the pram, the pram shifted but did not break its lashings, a sail lashed down on the foredeck was lost overboard. But by the time the next sea arrived, *Moonraker* had thrown the first one out, and we took the hint and hove to.

Rather dazed by all this battering we went below. The stove was out, the bunks were soaked, and while Ronnie was re-lighting the fire he was thrown violently against the wireless set, bruising a rib.

The whine of the wind, the crash of the seas, the rattle of spray like a distant burst of machine-gun fire, the concentration of thought, the physical force of moving uphill from the starboard side to the port, squatting on the slippery floor with a couple of tins and a pan, having forgotten to get the opener, hoping that someone filled the Primus after breakfast, but guessing they didn't and finding your guess was right.

The dim cabin (for a sail has been lashed between the pram and the cabin top to prevent more water coming through the skylights), the smell of wet clothes swinging in time to the ship's motion in front of the smoking fire, the knowledge that the gale is blowing you back the way you'd fought to come and that Ronnie's leave is up tomorrow night.

But the sea is for sailing, and this is a sailor's life. Hot stew and mugs of coffee are heartening things, and we turn in to get what sleep we can.

The blow was as short as it was fierce. A day later found us just inside the Juan de Fuca Strait becalmed on a long swell left over from the gale, and wishing for a friendly fishing-boat bound for Victoria that would take Ronnie home. Ronnie was working at the engine, when I saw *White Hart* making towards us. Never have the "Watch dogs of the Juan de Fuca Strait" as Tony and Bridget style themselves, been such a welcome sight, for Ronnie would be in Victoria that night.

Tony came out of his deckhouse.

"Where were you in that blow?" he hailed. "It blew sixty knots and eighty in the Hecate Strait, and it's the worst they've had on the coast in July for fifty years."

CHAPTER SIXTEEN

BRIEF INTERLUDE

DURING the winter Christopher had earned enough to travel across the United States by Greyhound bus, had worked his way back to England, spent a couple of months at home, booked a passage to Hudson Bay in a cargo steamer and had come down from Churchill by train.

He arrived at Victoria in August laden with ship's gear from King's at Burnham and a couple of jibs from Sadler's, which he managed to put through the Customs as ship's stores, and just in time to help put the finishing touches to the ship before the start of her long voyage home.

Moonraker had not been out of the water for eleven months and I suspected her bottom was a trifle dirty. Round the waterline the copper was riddled with pin-point holes and was thin as a sheet of paper. We had just decided to scrub at the Royal Victoria Yacht Club, when *Aura*, a small American sloop, sailed in. This in itself was so rare an event, for few Americans have the patience to sail in light winds or in a restricted anchorage, that I asked them aboard. Before they left Norman Blanchard said:

"You folks must come and visit with us at Seattle."

I explained that we should be on our way south in a few days.

"Look, Peter," said Norman, "I heard you say you had to scrub the bottom, why not haul her out at my yard on Union Lake? It won't cost you a dime."

I hesitated; not because all this might delay our departure but because, after less than two hours' acquaintance, Norman was offering me such a golden opportunity.

He said, "You can give a talk to the Seattle Yacht Club, and if there's work to be done you can pay me out of that. Call me before you leave Victoria."

In light winds and in thick weather we sailed across the Juan de Fuca Strait to Port Townsend, arriving at midnight. At eight o'clock the next morning I went along to clear for the U.S.A., and to my astonishment was hailed by a familiar voice. *Aura* had come to meet us. More than that, a motor-vessel had come to help to tow us. It was a triumphal procession that steamed all the thirty-eight miles up Puget Sound and locked into the Union Lake around which the city of Seattle is built.

Norman said he'd never seen anything like *Moonraker* in his life. Her full bilges, her fine run and her deep draught, her massive rudder fittings, all intrigued him.

He said, "I wouldn't have credited that a ship of her age could have kept her shape so well."

Nor could we understand how she could have sailed at all, so thick were the barnacles on her bottom.

Never have we scrubbed in such comfort. We scraped off the barnacles and washed her down with a hose. Norman came along with a huge tin of grease.

"Here, Peter, rub this all over her and she'll stay cleaner a bit longer. Now, what about this copper? Friend of mine at Pacific Marine said if I cared to come along he had some lying around the yard he didn't want. Now I come to look at it, there's enough to do your waterline."

The week we stayed at Seattle it rained most of the time, making the city look a little drab. I was taken over the Medico-Dental building that had just been added to the University of Washington. It is built in the contemporary style and is not without a certain practical beauty of its own, and it is, as you can imagine, magnificently equipped. The young professor who showed me round took me into the students' common-room, spacious and restful. I congratulated him on having such a pleasant place to relax.

"Relax!" he cried. "Our stoodents don't relax, Doctor, they work. We reckon we have five per cent of nervous breakdowns in a year."

One night the Blanchards asked us up to dinner on our own. There was a sensibility about Norman that does not often sit hand in hand with the feverish life of an American business-man, and we enjoyed that evening more than most, but when we left Eunice said to Anne:

"We feel so selfish not sharing you, but for just this once we wanted to have you to ourselves."

I went to see Norman in his office next day with my pockets full of dollars from the talk. I asked him for his bill.

He said, "My directors (I didn't know he had any) tell me that we've had so much publicity over you with the radio and T.V. that it's going down on the expense sheet. I'm not sure we shouldn't pay you!"

It was a wonderful feeling having a clean ship. We left Port Townsend on the beginning of the ebb and slipped out over the smooth sea with wraiths of fog drifting in from the strait until it became impossible to see the bowsprit end from the helm. The diaphone on New Dungeness Point brought back memories of the Sunk on a hot misty day in the Thames Estuary (how far away that seemed!) and we groped our way in behind a low spit of land which does in fact recall to mind Dungeness itself.

What a sail we had that night! The wind fresh from the west, the tide pouring down the Strait deceiving me by the pace it carried us up to windward, Anne's brilliant notion of counting the sequence of the red light for which I was so boldly steering to find it was Albert Head, a full eight miles to the west, the wild rush into the calm waters of the harbour nearly missing Fisherman's Wharf altogether, so unusual an appearance did it present. It was empty!

One or two of the seiners fishing off Active Pass (in the Gulf Islands) had intercepted a run of salmon making for the Fraser River. Within a very short time eighteen boats were hauling in fish as fast as it was humanly possible to do so. The Victoria to Vancouver steamer was confronted by a mass of lights, nets across the pass and a bunch of fishermen too busy to curse them as they tried to hoot their way through.

"This is our night, pal," they said. "You'll have to wait."

By breakfast time a million salmon had been caught, and as salmon was retailing at two dollars fifty a fish a few men had made a large number of dollars in a night.

There was, as you may well imagine, considerable rejoicing at Victoria that night. We had been out to dinner and were walking down the float when we noticed an Indian weaving uncertainly about the dock. By law no Indian is allowed to be served with alcohol, but this one had obviously been able to get around this tiresome regulation. As he was carrying a rifle under his shoulders we made a hasty retreat to our ship having, we hoped, escaped his notice.

We slipped below, drawing the curtain. The next thing I knew was that the curtain was thrust aside and the muzzle of a rifle was pointing at my middle.

A voice whispered, "White man come out."

The others, not in a direct line of fire, crept forward on a plan of their own, while I stayed there hoping that either the rifle was not loaded or that the Indian's fingers would not fumble too closely with the trigger. I thought I heard Anne slip out of the fo'c'sle and at that moment the barrel wandered away.

What happened next was a sort of anti-climax. I jerked the barrel to one side, Christopher joined me, Anne took the Indian in the rear but there was nothing there to fight. He was just like a dish full of jelly, limp and cold. We took the bolt out of the rifle (it was not loaded) and dragged him back to his seiner. In the morning I went round to return the bolt to the skipper but the ship had gone so when he next takes that rifle out of the rack to shoot a deer, he'll get a surprise!

Before we sailed I had a letter from Bill Priest of *Tara*. You may remember that we had last seen him steaming out of Musgrave Cove on his way south to Seattle and then to San Francisco. Some months later we had heard through the ocean voyager's grapevine that *Tara* had been lost, a rumour that was afterwards contradicted but, as there is rarely smoke without a fire, we had wondered what had given rise to it. In this letter Bill told us his story:

They had left the Juan de Fuca Strait rather later than he had intended and had been caught in a sou'-easter in which the main gaff and the steel jackstay had carried away, the mizzen sail split and *Tara* was driven many miles off her course. That the gale blew along the coast and not on to it undoubtedly saved their lives.

The gale blew itself out and, as so often happens in these waters, was succeeded by days of calm. They motored down the Oregon coast and arrived off Gray's Harbour at night. *Tara's* people were desperately tired and the one thing they wanted was to set foot on dry land; but Bill had no large-scale charts of the harbour or of the river beyond. He rang up the coastguards on the ship-to-shore radio and was told that it was safe to come in as it was nearly high water, so he negotiated the entrance and motored up the river. Unfortunately he mistook a light that was in the middle of a rocky patch for that on a lighted buoy and at five knots with the flood-tide under him he ran *Tara* right up on the rocks, ripping a considerable part of her port side out of her. To most of us *Tara* would have appeared a total loss, but not to Bill. With the help of the coastguards he got hold of some empty oil-drums and, as the tide went down and the water poured out of her hull, they cut down the bulkheads with axes, enlarged the opening to the hatch and packed the hull with the empty drums. They tacked a sail over the torn hull and arranged for a launch to stand by as the flood returned.

Tara floated. The launch took her in tow, but on their way up to the shipyard the pressure of air below started to lift the cabin top so there were Bill and his crew hammering in nails for all they were worth to prevent the sea from wresting victory from their grasp—and they won! But, as Bill said in his letter, how much less exhausted they would have been if they had spent one night more at sea.

Some weeks later I met Bill at Newport, California. He looked, although this may have been my imagination, an older man.

He said, "You know, Peter, there's still a lot I've got to learn about the sea."

CHAPTER SEVENTEEN

THROUGH THE GOLDEN GATE

PROFITING by Bill's unfortunate experience in *Tara* we made up our minds to keep a hundred miles off the coast of Oregon on our way to San Francisco. By doing so we should avoid the constant north-westerly current running up the coast and gain some advantage, perhaps, from the warm Japanese current running in the opposite direction.

With this plan in mind we left Port Renfrew (a pub and a dozen houses climbing up a hill), and as the ship rose to the swell our hearts rose too, for we were homeward bound after two years. The day was fine and sunny, and as we reached the Light and Whistle buoy a salmon troller, a stranger to us, came up at high speed. While her owner kept the boat a few feet away his wife threw a prince of fish upon our decks.

"Good luck," she cried. "Give my love to the Old Country when you get back!"

The wind fell light, and all night we sailed or drifted over a quiet sea, and at dawn we were only just outside the strait. It was as if *Moonraker* was reluctant to leave.

Light head winds, sudden squalls and torrential rain were our lot until we were within three hundred miles of San Francisco. Here we were so utterly becalmed that it seemed as if the world had run out of wind. The sun beat down upon our decks from a cloudless sky.

The following afternoon I came up on deck, sleepy-eyed, and at first I could see nothing except the long north-westerly swell, until I noticed a few pale blue whorls like the paws of a cat spreading away from the ship in an ever-widening circle. A faint air came from the north-west, the ship stirred, and before I had time to guy the boom and set the spinnaker (the others were deep in their afternoon sleep) the circle had grown till its form was lost and a breeze had been born again. It grew into a healthy child that night and into a lustier one next day. On the following morning my meridian sight gave me rather a

British Columbia to Panama

shock. We were too far to the west. How humiliating it would be if the current and the surface drift from this fine wind whisked us past San Francisco before we could make in to the land! The breeze, now two days old, was Force 7 on the Beaufort scale and under reefed staysail and four-reefed main we hauled in the sheets and made for the land. It was Anne's watch and if she did not complain it was from force of circumstance rather than from a stoical nature. Whenever she opened her mouth half the Pacific Ocean tried to slip past her throat.

"Good practice," I told her from under the shelter of the hatch, "for crossing the Caribbean."

My noon position showed there was little need for my panic and as soon as it was my turn to go on watch we ran before the wind with dry decks. At ten o'clock that night I climbed the ratlines and saw the flash of Point Reyes Lighthouse fine on the port bow twenty-five miles away. Behind this point lies Drake's Bay where Sir Francis came to an anchor in June of 1580 after giving up his attempt to find a way round North America. Hakluyt records. :

We found the ayre so cold, that our men being grievously pinched with the same, complained of the extremities thereof, and the further we went, the more the colde increased upon us. Wherefore we thought it best for that time to seeke the land, and did so, finding it not mountainous, but low, plaine land within 38 degrees of the line. In which height it pleased God to send us into a faire and good Baye, with a good winde to enter the same.

We followed Drake's example, beating into this "faire and good Baye" as the eastern sky began to lighten. Gone were the dripping pines of the British Columbian coast and in their place the smooth rounded hills looked, in that pre-morning light, remarkably like our Sussex Downs. We hoisted the yellow flag and went to sleep.

The ship snubbing at her chain woke me up. Hard squalls came down from the north, a white mist, as cold as a wraith, blew eerily past the ship and the diaphone on Point Reyes Lighthouse emphasized my thankfulness that we were not at this moment groping our way into the Golden Gate. It was

noon before we sailed. In patches of clearing mist the red-
brown cliffs of the coast flew past, but by the time we rounded
Bonita Point the Golden Gate, the noble span of the bridge
and the white city of San Francisco, shining in the sun, burst
upon us with the same impact that Desolation Sound had done
a thousand miles to the north.

This was to be, I had thought, one of the big moments of
my life, but if an onlooker had been stationed on the bridge he
would, alas, have seen no stately sailing ship winging in from
sea but a reefed-down gaff-cutter that appeared to tack down-
wind. For one of these disagreements which break out in the
best regulated yachts (forgive me if I am wrong, but I think
they probably do) was in full swing. Christopher had friends
at Sausalito on the north side of the bay; I maintained we
should "clear" at San Francisco on the south side, and Anne,
who has never had the slightest reverence for authority, said
that was silly. As arguments were hurled across the decks so
did the ship point first to San Francisco and then to Sausalito.

Of course we went to Sausalito, and naturally no one took
the slightest notice of our yellow flag. The U.S.A. officials are
not always partial to yachtsmen, and I dared not go ashore;
so in desperation I rowed into the Yacht Basin, looking lost,
until the master of a motor yacht asked what I wanted.

I told him.

"I can get the Customs on my 'phone," he said. "I'll speak
to the boss."

In a moment or two I was speaking to the boss myself.

"I hear you've come a long way to see us," said a pleasant
voice. "I'll send a man over to clear you in the morning."

I rowed back to the ship. Christopher and Anne had dinner
waiting for me. Not by so much as the flicker of an eyelid did
they betray their evident content. Afterwards, being well fed,
I went up on deck. There was a flat calm and a thousand lights
were reflected upon the water. Our breeze, just over three days
old, had died.

Americans say that there are three cities in their country
that are worth a visit, New York, New Orleans and San Francisco. San Francisco is built, like Rome, on many hills, up and

down which we rode, like children out on a treat, on cable cars. In the evening, as we walked along the almost deserted business section, the narrow streets, the massive stone buildings, reminded us of Leadenhall Street on a Sunday afternoon.

It has the largest Chinatown outside China and, like all great cities, its slums and hide-outs, but the sad part of San Francisco is the harbour.

In the museum there are photographs of the bay studded with full-rigged ships waiting to load, but from Telegraph Hill this morning we saw, in all these miles of docks, two ships; both of them sound asleep. Strikes and lock-outs were responsible for this; the work, we were told, of one man who had successfully driven the trade southwards to San Pedro, the port for Los Angeles. It was to be hoped, they said, that he would go there too and drive it back again.

Down in the fish harbour at night the place still comes alive. The garish lights, the honky-tonks, the canned music and the rattle of plates bring to mind what San Francisco must have been like at the turn of this century. Here the spirit of the sea still lives; in the sturdy lines of the fishing craft, in the men who sail out in search of salmon or who hunt the albacore down to the coast of Mexico. Mr Gann, in *Fiddler's Green*, gives you the feeling of the waterfront, or what is left of it, far better than I can.

Facing you, as you come in from the Golden Gate, is the Island of Alcatraz. It is small and is almost entirely covered by the huge stone buildings of the prison. On the chart it is surrounded by red lines inside which no vessel may penetrate. When fog comes rolling in through the Golden Gate (as it does four days out of seven at this time of the year) you can hear the horn on the lighthouse sounding its dismal warning to the free and its chance of freedom to the prisoner; but it is the boast of the authorities that no man has ever escaped from Alcatraz and lived.

While San Francisco hides her head in fog Sausalito basks in the sun. It is small, and the buildings straggling up the street reminded us of Sesimbra in Portugal. Christopher's friends, whose house overlooked the harbour, drove us up the Napa

Valley where grow the finest grapes, according to the San Franciscans, in California. We visited an American wine lodge. A rather bored middle-aged man took us round. From his remarks I gathered they had no time to waste in letting wine mature so they first extracted the elements of natural processes, "hotted 'em up" and finally re-injected them. We tasted but saw no reason to buy.

We went on to an Italian wine lodge. It was a family affair. A man with the look of a Lombardy peasant in his eye introduced us to others of his family (first-generation Americans), discoursed about wines, comparing theirs with those of Italy, and told us that here there was little difference in their methods. The grapes were crushed by machines (no peasants' feet allowed in this asceptic country) but otherwise the juices were allowed to ferment in their natural way. The wine tasted good, and we bought as much as we could conveniently stow aboard our ship.

On the only afternoon that we had set aside for work on the ship (for San Franciscans are a hospitable lot) a man came hobbling down the float on crutches, his right foot so swathed in bandages that I took this, quite wrongly, to be a case of gout. He was short and stocky with a pointed grey beard. Hilary Belloc described himself as a "Mender of Roads" but in a less mechanical age he might have been one of the great entertainers like the late Mr Percy French.

A few days ago Hilary had been inspecting a manhole. As he lifted the heavy cover he said to himself, "Now, don't drop this on your foot."

"Blow me," said Hilary, "I forgot all about the bloody thing and dropped it on my foot."

Hilary and Nevil Shute who was over from Australia, were thinking of going down to the Big Sur country in a few days, and they asked us to come with them. Hilary's entire luggage for the three days consisted of a case of red wine and two straw hats.

The road kept close to the coast with occasional detours round hills while the Pacific thundered on rocks or surged into sandy bays.

We lunched at Monterey. Cannery Row was deserted. Where was the Palace Flop House, the Bear Flag, Suzy's Boiler and Western Biological? I do not know, for I had not the courage to go and find out.

Farther south we had a look at Carmel Mission, the oldest on the Coast, but Carmel had been "hotted up" like the American wine, and retained about as much feeling as a downtown drugstore. Only the tower and the belfry had been left alone.

When we had disentangled ourselves from curios, mementoes and hordes of automobiles, we drove to Point Lobos, watching the famous cypress trees waving in the breeze, drove down the "Seventeen Mile Drive" (where people built houses on the same scale as Palm Beach) and had tea in Pebble Beach. The village is "cute"; Olde Worlde Shoppes, and a house, so Hilary said, that had all its plumbing done in gold. On the walls of the Bank there is a plaque showing Friar Sierra running through a wrought-iron grille with the worried expression of a client that has been refused an overdraft.

We headed south to the Big Sur Country. It used to be a haunt for people who wanted to get as close to nature and as far from their fellow men as possible, but since the highway has been built it is on its way to becoming California's greatest "Back to Nature" attraction. It has fluted mountain ridges, deep valleys and a climate as good as most. We left the highway and drove up a narrow dirt track which rose in spirals until we looked down upon the Pacific from a great height. The noise of the engine disturbed young deer which bounded in great leaps into the bush, and we came in time to the bungalow of Henry Miller, the author. He was out. A soft wind blew in from the Pacific Ocean sixteen hundred feet below, and the heat haze that had given this rugged coastline an ethereal look slowly disappeared. Mountains, valleys and sea became hard and real and there was no trace of a human hand.

We never met Mr Miller, but I read an article of his quite recently on the Big Sur Country. He writes:

I have come to take a different view of it however . . . Yes, I can visualize vast multitudes living where there are now only a few scattered families. There is room for thousands upon thousands to come . . . There will be airplanes, seaplanes, helicopters . . . An isolated Paradise may be good for the soul but the Paradise which belongs to all because it is made by all is the one we long to inherit . . .

A brave New World, in fact?

We got back into the car and climbed still higher till we came to a wood on the summit of a ridge. Here we were met by eight horses and a veritable giant of a man whose pale face was framed in a long black beard. His stare was neither hostile nor friendly but wary, as Man Friday's might have been till he got to know Crusoe better. To Hilary's questions he returned monosyllabic answers, allowing us to pass on our way to his cottage with a nod of his head. This cottage had been built by a Spanish gynaecologist, a friend of Hilary's, who had subsequently died of drink. Everything was of concrete, walls, floor, a great fireplace and a huge double bed where the gynaecologist slept on straw. He was a mystic who was given to fits of violent remorse, and in one of these he had lit a fire in the middle of the room and then had torn a hole in the ceiling to let out the smoke. He was a man of great personal charm when he was sober and was most attractive to women. The fact that none of them lasted very long may have had something to do with the bed. Hilary, striding about this large, untidy room, talked about the place in Jaime's time while a woman, silently and efficiently, fried hamburgers for her son. At length he decided that his hostess, whose guests were none of her choosing, might have other things to do, so we took our leave.

Of the man we had met at the gate there was no sign.

Our way home took us through a redwood grove and we got out to see the trees; but the thing I remember is Hilary tramping down a sunlit path declaiming Housman in his strong, clear voice. He took the Highway Number One back to San Francisco, past artichoke fields, lettuces in orderly rows in gargantuan flat fields where packing vans and men were almost unseen in all this distance.

Every few miles there were vast hoardings on which were

pictured a happy American family with the words YOU ARE LUCKY TO LIVE IN AMERICA underneath it. It was, I think, part of an advertisement for someone's beer, but it seemed to me it might serve a double purpose. If I had to look at that month after month, year after year, it might almost make me believe it.

CHAPTER EIGHTEEN

THE COAST OF CALIFORNIA

A SPARKLING wind filled our sails as we sped down the coast from San Francisco at a greater speed, so it seemed to us, than that at which we had motored down it a few days ago. Measuring our runs in days instead of hours we were content to let the roaring bow wave and the curving mast seduce our senses into thinking that time was relative, and at dawn on our first morning out the Big Sur Country looked strangely mysterious, for the tops of the highest mountains, hard and brown like a distant ridge in the Sahara desert, stood out above a veil of mist as though it were a mirage a hundred miles away.

If we had known that this was to be the last good breeze we should have for the next three months our high spirits, as we rounded Point Concepcion (two hundred miles to the south and locally and grandiloquently known as the Cape Horn of the North Pacific owing to the difficulty of rounding it against the fresh north-west wind and the current) would have been more than an octave lower.

At dawn we lay a mile or so off Santa Barbara harbour becalmed in a thick fog. Christopher, for about the twentieth time, suggested it was time to start the engine, but since we had unseized it with infinite trouble at Port Renfrew without finding out why it had seized up, I was determined to use it only for an emergency. But Christopher's doleful expression (he had a girl friend waiting for him here) was too much for me. We cranked it up, the breakwater and the buoys marking the sand spit to port came into view, but within two hundred yards of our berth the poor thing developed a rattle in its throat that was all too realistic and died.

Poor Christopher! There was no shore leave. With blood and sweat, amid oil and filth, we levered the heavy engine out, rigged a sling and with a handy billy guided it on to the deck. Even to my unmechanical eye there was something very definitely wrong. A neighbouring yachtsman who had given us a hand and much good advice told us nonchalantly that to put in a new front bearing, which was the cause of the trouble, would cost not less than two hundred and fifty dollars; a hundred pounds!

We were given an introduction to Mr G. In his spare time G. was a big-game hunter. He had the shoulders of an ox, a great square head, a lined and pitted skin rather like the rhinos he may have chased, but in amongst the folds of flesh two merry eyes shone out and belied his otherwise ferocious aspect. He listened to our story in an amused, off-hand sort of a way:

"I've no time to do your engine," he said, "but I'll come and see your boat." In silence he looked at our spars and gear and took in the small, untidy cabin with a wry smile. He said, "If you're so crazy as to come out from England in this I guess I'd better fix your engine."

I explained our predicament more fully: "We've only got a small dollar reserve but the Bank of England will send yachtsmen money for repairs, up to a certain amount, if they get an estimate of the work involved."

He nodded. "Come and see me around noon, to-morrow."

The next morning we met him over the body of our engine.

"Fifty dollars too much for you?" he asked, and when I started to speak he went on, "Pays my man's wages, that's all I want."

The work was to be completed by Saturday, and on that day we all trooped down to fetch it. Along with the new main-bearing, new big-ends and other improvements G. had thrown in a gallon of oil and a bagful of handsome rags, the sort of rags Anne and I could dress ourselves in!

He said, "Jim, here (Jim was his mechanic), wants to help you put it in."

When we protested that this was entirely unnecessary, he smiled. "He doesn't want to be paid for it, he just wants to see it running. He can do what he wants with his week-end."

This, indeed, was providential, for as soon as we had bedded the monster down (it is only six-horsepower, but it feels like a ton weight) Jim clutched the exhaust-pipe a shade too tightly so that it crumpled to rust in his hand. From somewhere he found another for three dollars; and on Sunday night it ran with more sweetness than it had for several years. Jim did not drink, neither did he smoke, and it was as much as we could do to feed him, so anxious was he not to denude our ship of stores, of which he thought we might be in need.

I said, "Jim, you've been very good to us, surely there's something we can do for you in return."

"There sure is," he replied. "Send me a postcard when you get back."

Now it was not only on account of Christopher that we had come to Santa Barbara. While at Honolulu we had met the Kelloggs who had invited us to stay at their ranch on our way south. Although we were a year late and Irma was now in Arizona, she had repeated this offer, insisting that we stayed at the ranch until she could join us.

The Rancho Monte Alegre lies behind Carpentaria, some twelve miles to the east of Santa Barbara in the foothills of the mountains. Under a cloudless sky the place lives in a little world of its own among acres of lemon trees worked by Mexicans. Beneath a row of tall palm trees stands the graceful one-storeyed ranch house and the guest cottage where Ian and Betty Dewar live and where we lived too until Irma arrived. Farther down the slope was the bunkhouse. This had been converted by Pete (Irma's son-in-law) who lived there and kept a watchful eye on the Mexican workers, while Joan, for whose sake Christopher had begged me to start the engine, lived opposite in what had once been the office. She shared this with seven (or was it seventeen?) cats.

While in Santa Barbara the white buildings and the broad streets swam in the heat of the noon-day sun, and at night the restaurants reverberated to the shouts of Mexican singers and American saxophones, we lay in Betty's garden, or by the shores of a tiny lake at the upper end of the ranch. We came to know them well.

Both Pete and Ian had been fliers, Pete in the last and Ian in the first war. Seeing little future in the R.A.F. in the late twenties Ian had taken a job with a Canadian air-line and come out with his wife and two children, but before he arrived the air-line had gone bankrupt.

He told me how he had joined a charter firm, and for the next year and a half he flew people from province to province, from town to town.

"Talking to you like this," he remarked, "has reminded me of a queer little incident just before the Wall Street crash. A client of ours approached me personally to fly him on a special mission because, he said, I knew how to keep my mouth shut. Although this was against the regulations the boss suggested that for such an excellent client (he was a doctor who was reputed to have made a fortune out of performing illegal operations) I should fall in with his wishes. We set off about mid-day and he told me to follow the Red River up into the mountains behind. The country was wild and rugged, but the doctor indicated to me a valley at the head of which was a grassy plateau where we landed without difficulty.

"We walked to a clearing where there were buildings, but what puzzled me more than these—and how they could have got there—was the low continuous roar of machines. It was a noise faintly familiar, but before I could think what it reminded me of the doctor had hustled me into an office, where I was introduced to one of the most powerful men I have ever seen. Hirsute, I suppose you'd call him; his face was covered in black beard and under his open shirt was a growth like the Black Forest. He spoke to me in execrable French, but when he and the doctor conversed I couldn't understand a word they were saying although, again, the sound was vaguely familiar.

"After the doctor had finished his business he said, 'I shan't be coming back tonight, but this gentleman's son wishes to travel with you.' The young man was nearly as big as his father, but spoke good English. I told him he'd freeze to death in his shirt sitting in an open cockpit but he refused to put on as much as an overcoat. He never turned a hair."

I said, "And the noise?"

"A printing press."

"The language?"

"Russian."

Pete drove us down to Hollywood in the station-wagon, and we had the experience of being driven on the Los Angeles Freeway, where cars fly in and out like tracer bullets, and the minimum speed is 55 m.p.h.

Pete says it is the safest road in the U.S.A., but Pete is used to battles in the air and we are not. We dined at Don the Beachcomber's under three paintings by Le Tec lit by coloured lights in blown-out porcupine-fish, eating delicate Chinese food and drinking Barbados rum. We were back in bed on the ranch before dawn.

In the meantime gangs of painters, decorators and Mexican women were busy preparing the ranch house for Irma's arrival. Long-distance telephones, telegrams and letters changed and counter-changed the moment of her coming. Then one day she just appeared.

Descended from a Norwich sea-captain and a Spanish señorita, Irma is a remarkable woman with a low, husky voice. In spite of being a grandmother, she has the grace of a Spanish dancing-girl, her long black hair falling over her shoulders. She hides an acute business sense behind a façade of girlishness, but she is one of the most generous people we have ever met.

Irma spared us a week.

Thinking we could do some little thing in return for her hospitality, we asked her whether she would like to see our colour slides and hear something of our travels.

"That would be lovely," she said, "I'll ask some friends in after dinner and share the pleasure with them."

She asked about thirty and it was nearly midnight by the time the party was over. Irma came up to Anne and me. She said, "My friends were so delighted they wished me to give you this small token to show their appreciation." The "token" covered the cost of the engine, and this reversal of my intentions made me blush to the roots of my hair.

On the day she left she made two appointments in the town, and not one of the twenty-five people who had come to see her off (so unerring is her instinct for collecting round her devotees of both sexes) would have given any odds on her catching that

train. The great engine puffed into the station, Ian rushed off
to try and bribe the guard to wait a little longer when Irma
stepped radiantly on to the platform with hatboxes, trunks and
several minor slaves to carry her things. She kissed the women-
folk, accepted our trifling gifts as if they were myrrh and in-
cense and was wafted away towards Arizona.

The passage to Newport, California, is a distance of only a
hundred and twenty miles, but it took us three days. The mist
hung on, and for a day and a night we navigated by the sound
of the traffic along the coast road, coming about, for the wind
was ahead, when the roar grew too loud, and again when it
had almost ceased. But we kept an eye on a motoring map,
for at times the road went inland behind hills!

An acquaintance of ours had had an accident in this very
part of the world. He was an Australian whom we had met at
Honolulu and again, much to our surprise, in Vancouver City.
He had, he told us, been given the job of taking one of the
ocean racers back to San Pedro. They had made their landfall
at Santa Barbara and a day or two later they had left, as we
had done, in mist and with only the lightest of airs. They set
off under power, adjusted the automatic pilot to a course that
would take them between Anacapa and the mainland and
retired below. Some hours later our friend came up on deck
with a bowl of soup in his hands and there, right in front of his
nose, were the cliffs of Anacapa. Before he could put down his
soup they hit the beach.

"Coo," he said. "Sixty thousand dollars down the drain."

Not having an automatic pilot, we negotiated the channel
successfully, but the passage was not without its perils. Between
Point Huamine and Point Dune was a guided-missile range
which extended an unspecified depth to seaward (probably
about sixteen miles) from a mile offshore. It was, however,
never used at night. We took no chances and navigated this
sheet of water within half a mile of the shore and at night.
Again, crossing San Pedro bay all the tuna clippers in the world
seemed to be homeward bound from the fishing grounds off
Peru. One of them came so close that we could see a small seaplane, like a crouching insect, on her afterdeck. The thump of

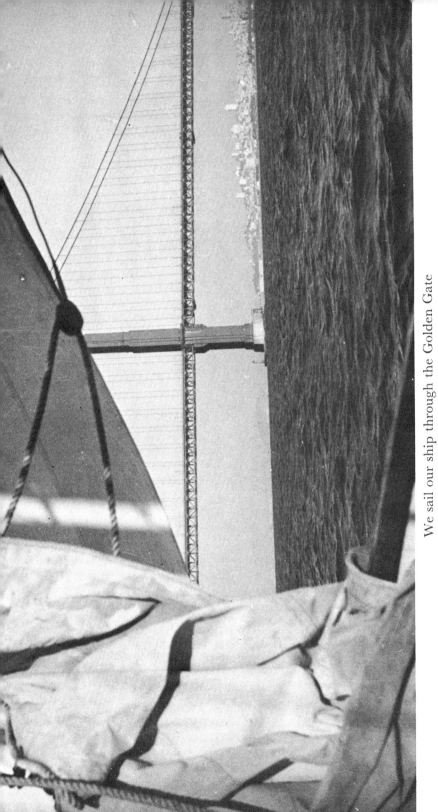

We sail our ship through the Golden Gate

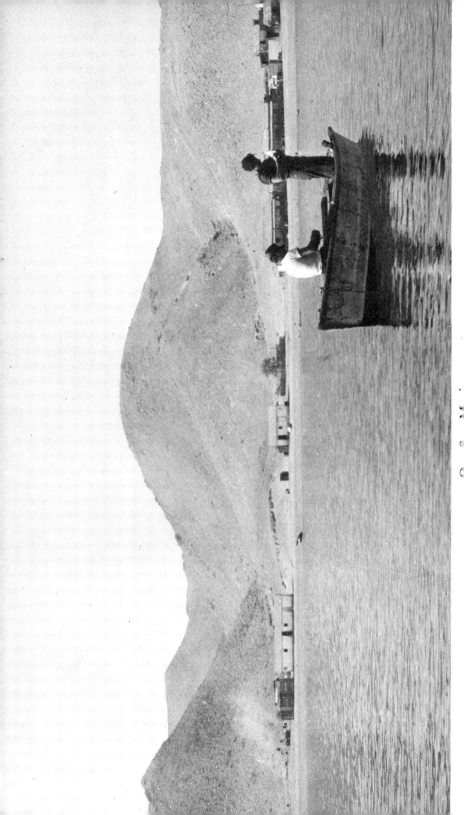

their powerful engines, the cluster of lights about their enormous superstructures and the hiss of their bow waves kept us on the look-out until just before dawn. Then there was fog.

Entering Newport was like sailing into a Dutch canal, with houses right down to the waterside and creeks winding into the flat and featureless shore. Yachts by the thousand lay at anchor, but in spite of this gross overcrowding there was a peace about the place that appealed to our imagination. As we drew alongside the Newport Harbor Yacht Club someone came running out of the Clubhouse and said that Dr. Pye was wanted on the telephone and was I he? Peggy Slater had seen our sails from a friend's house as we beat up the channel. Could we, she asked, come and have dinner at their house? We most certainly could.

Peggy is a yacht broker from San Pedro whom we had seen in Barbados, met in Honolulu and again in Santa Barbara. She lives in a bungalow at San Pedro right on top of a cliff, and a single plate-glass window runs the whole length of the living room overlooking the Pacific Ocean. A ship's wheel for a table, coral shells and fans round the walls, the model of a four-masted barque and a glorious divan where Anne and I once spent a blissful night watching the firelight on the redwood ceiling and listening to the murmur of the sea on the beach two hundred feet below.

Peggy was one of the few women we met on this coast who was a seaman in her own right. She took us sailing one day in her K.38. Anne was at the helm and Peggy and I were below talking about the ships we had known and heard about. Suddenly she broke off in the middle of a sentence and glanced out of the hatch at a vessel tearing down under a press of engine.

"Give this thing a wide berth, Anne," she said. "There's an awful lot of inexperience on that ship."

But it is as an ocean-racing skipper that Peggy is best known. Some years ago she was sailing master of *Apache* in the Trans-Pacific race. The *Apache* was running with her whole mainsail and a web spinnaker before half a gale of wind when the cry went up: "Man overboard!"

Peggy was on deck in a flash. Someone had thrown the man

a lifebuoy with a smoke attachment, but the seas were so big that in this short time all sight of him had been lost. Peggy came to the conclusion that to gybe with that spinnaker set would dismast the vessel, so down it had to come, and by that time they had run a mile.

Peggy said, "I needed all my know-how. I had a man on the lower spreaders, and I could hear the screams from the poor guy's sister, who had to be held down in her bunk by more men than I could willingly spare from the deck. At one time we were less than two hundred yards away, but in the sea then running we failed to see him. It must have seemed incredible to him when we turned away."

They searched for twenty-nine hours. At the end of that time the captain of the escort ship that had joined in the search said he had orders to proceed with the rest of the fleet and that *Apache* must also continue. Peggy refused. Backwards and forwards went the argument (for by now the sea was smooth), and at last the captain agreed to search for another two hours farther to the east, where Peggy's navigator thought the missing man might now be. An hour later he was found, alive!

Lying in the harbour of Newport was the schooner *Vega* which we had last seen at Papeete. She was being entirely re-fitted for a passenger service from Honolulu to Tahiti, and her crew were from the South Seas: from Atuona, the Paumotus and the Societies. We brought wine, someone produced a guitar, and in a moment houses, yachts, cars, dollars and even the American language vanished, and we were back among the waving palms, the dusky maidens and the murmur of the sea upon the reef.

As we walked back that night we believed more strongly than ever that MacDonald the painter had been right: these were no children who, if given the chance, would reach out for the benefits of a Western State. They were as adult as we were, loving their way of life.

We sailed in company with Hale Field and his wife in their gaff-topsail cutter *Renegade* in the usual mist and light winds. On Saturday night a fog came down. I woke to hear Anne talking in a conversational manner to Hale. I was out in a moment. Although I could see nothing at all, I could hear the crash of *Renegade's* boom as she rolled in the swell. Both ships were becalmed, and as there was nothing to be done I went below. The desultory conversation went on and on and on, and I hoped Hale's crew were better at sleeping than I was.

Christopher had a smart breeze from ahead in his watch, but in mine it petered out. When that happens I curl up on the cabin floor and snatch some sleep. It is not a thing I encourage in the others, and my excuse is that at the slightest change in the weather or at the beat of a steamer's engines I shall wake up. But on this occasion a breeze sprang up unannounced; and with a feeling of guilt I found the ship sailing merrily back the way she had come, while *Renegade*, whose crew had stuck to their duty, was almost out of sight. Now in all the years that I have indulged in this unorthodox practice I have never been caught by my crew, but I had more than a little difficulty in explaining to Christopher why *Renegade*, which had been well astern when he went off watch, was now so far ahead.

At San Diego, big, noisy, and rather inaccessible from the harbour, there lay in a neglected corner of the dockyard half a dozen boats and a band of sea adventurers who had founded the first international cruising association. The only qualification is that you must live aboard a sea-going vessel and cruise when you are able. You might describe them as the core of those Americans, some of whom we had already met in the South Pacific, who sail from country to country, from continent to continent, turning their hands to any job until their finances recover sufficiently to continue their marine prowling about the world. They came from a cross-section of the population, they were individualists scorning what they called the "rat-race", bound to each other by the ties of the sea, independent, self-reliant, abhorred by the bureaucrats but the cream of the earth, no doubt, to Mr Geoffrey Household. They were the nearest thing to the Westerner's conception of South Sea Island life.

After a few days we went round and joined them. At the issue of the monthly bulletin we sat crowded into *Black Dolphin's* spacious cabin and fittingly enough there were letters from

Wanderer III from Capetown and from *Yankee* from the New Hebrides.

It was while we were at San Diego that the Los Angeles Yacht Club did me the honour of asking me to give them a talk at one of their lunches. Peggy drove us up to the city where we met a number of the Trans-Pacific ocean racing men and Dwight Long (of *Idle Hour* fame) who had recently been making a film in the South Sea Islands.

He was feeling depressed.

He said, "If I'd taken the advice of my friends and used professional actors instead of spending months trying to train the Tahitians it might have been a success."

After the talk a member got up and said, "Now we would like to hear something from Mrs Pye."

Anne, who hates talking because she says she never knows what her tongue is going to say next, stood up.

Someone asked, "Mrs Pye, can you tell us how we can get our wives to go to sea with us?"

Anne said, "Oh yes, I can tell you that at once. Don't keep them in the galley."

There was an awkward silence, and the meeting broke up in disorder. The word has evidently gone round, for Anne has never been asked to speak since!

No foreign yachtsman could, I think, come down this coast without being interviewed by television, by radio and the press; nor could he escape being visited by a great many people whose only interest in the ship is curiosity and to have something to talk to their friends about. It gave us quite a lot of amusement, and Anne one day heard a woman in our cabin say to a friend, "I saw Mrs Pye on T.V. She looked so tall and graceful and lovely, but of course T.V. is *so* deceptive, isn't it?"

CHAPTER NINETEEN

THE MAGIC OF MEXICO

WE sailed on a Sunday in November. The breeze was light
from the north-west, tempting us out. Night descended upon
us, a Joseph Conrad sort of night, dark and mysterious, Behind were the neon lights, the flashing lights, the roar of jets,
seaplanes and air-liners, while on the beam was the silence of
Mexico; nothing but the dim shapes of mountains, as remote as
Mars. To seaward a single light flickered, for it was Mexican
and therefore temperamental, on the Islas Coronados.

In her early morning watch Anne had cleared Los Coronados—"round dry humps sticking steeply out of the water"—
and was steering for Isla Guadalupe, unlit and uninhabited, a
hundred and fifty miles away. I first saw it two days later in the
pre-dawn light. The precipitous cliffs of its northern end rose
out of a veil of mist, softening their bold and rugged outlines;
and once more it came upon me that there can be no more
exciting thing than making a landfall in the middle of the sea.
The wind piped up, and I had to call the others to shorten sail.
The anchorage was in a small cove, a mile and a half from
North Point, and was hardly big enough to swing a cat in, and
our bowsprit was almost over the beach before we found the
bottom with the lead.

There was someone there after all; a fisherman poaching
lobsters for bait. He thought we were Mexicans and took to
the bush, but when we ran up our colours he came out with
half a dozen lobsters.

He said, "This is a goddam awful place. You roll like hell,
and if a sou'-easter comes up you have to get out at once."

Warming to his subject, he went on, "Looks a bit like that
now. I've seen a *chubasco* (Spanish for surprise storm) roll a
tuna boat over and drown her crew."

He downed a pint of beer.

He said, "Last year a boat got wrecked over on the west
coast. Took 'em fourteen days to scale the cliffs and walk seven

miles to this bay. Blow me, when they got to the top of that ridge over there they saw a tuna boat from San Pedro anchored right here. They got most of the way down when the fish-boat up-anchors and steams out. They were half-dying of thirst and lack of food and that kinda made 'em mad. They yelled and waved, and then one of 'em set fire to the bush. The skipper saw the smoke and picked 'em up. Were they lucky!"

To the south a long curving beach was occupied by giant elephant-seals, slimy and repulsive with red, open mouths and hooked noses. On a bluff were the ruins of a penal settlement. The silence was absolute except for the whoof of the seals.

As I look back on the weeks we spent off the Mexican coast, my recollections are of constantly searching the horizon for wind. Our standards fell so low that steerage way was dubbed "not too bad", and a light breeze became like a Trade Wind. There is a note in my journal that for nineteen hours the log spinner had not rotated for so much as half a turn, and we looked upon our topsail with the greatest affection.

But if the voyage was slow and irksome because we were pressed for time there were compensations. The unruffled sea, the warmth of the sun, putting the world to rights beneath a shining moon and over an after-dinner cup of coffee, and making a landfall so beautiful that the memory of it still sends a little prickle of appreciation down my spine. It appeared at dawn. A high mackerel sky, suffused with bands of brilliant red and mauve and purple, held my attention until my eyes dropped to the level of the horizon where, as in a fairy tale, I saw two distant mountains sitting on the very rim of the world. They were part of the outer ramparts that enclose Magdalena Bay, a peninsula composed of sand-dunes and low, flat country that divorces the place from its more fortunate neighbours.

The bay is an inland sea eighteen miles long by ten wide approached through a narrow opening; and on the sands of this lagoon are bones of dead whales bleached by the sun, for here they come to die. Round a point we came upon our first Mexican village, a collection of adobe huts covered with corrugated roofs, around which we could see no living thing.

Doffing his wide sombrero the Captain of the Port welcomed us to his puebla and started to bake us *tortillas* with his own hands. A pile of maize, a hollow in the middle of the pile, a little water in the hollow, the whole kneaded by strong, stubby fingers, flicked from hand to hand like cards by a conjuror, thinned and flattened, the while he beamed with pleasure at the rapt attention of his pupils; he then baked the *tortillas* on a griddle made of tin and previously heated in a kerosene can used as an oven. It looked so simple, but when Anne tried her hand, amid grins and "*buenas*," her *tortillas* bore no resemblance to the master's.

The great delicacy was tinned shark-meat in oil, and a tin was opened for us. Never have we had to work so hard to show a proper appreciation of such an honour.

The people had to fetch every drop of water from the water-hole half a mile to the northward, and if it hadn't been for the fish in the sea they would have starved. The only money they had was spent on beer, and by five o'clock most of the village was insensible, a thing you could hardly blame them for be-cause there was nothing else to do.

Our voyage continued. The rocks off Cabo San Lucas at the tip of the Bahia California reminded us of the Needles as they had done the Worshipful Thomas Cavendish of Trimly in Suffolk when he lay in wait for the yearly arrival of the Manila galleon in the *Desire* with the *Content* in close attendance. Thus he captured the *Santa Maria* and took her into Aguada in Bahia San Lucas where he put his prisoners ashore:

They were set ashore where they had a fayre river of fresh water, with great store of fresh fish, foule, and wood and also many hares and connies upon the maine land.

But the place seemed to have changed in the last four hun-dred years, for there was no "fayre river", no fish or hares or connies, but a canning factory and a temporary butcher's shop beneath a tree from which hung the remains of a slaughtered bullock. Children and dogs carried away the entrails under the predatory eyes of huge buzzards with great red heads waiting for the remains.

Anne took her shopping basket, and we walked along the long hot road to the puebla, a more modern affair than Puerta Magdalena, with a village square, a church, two shops and a profusion of red bougainvillea. A shy, gentle population, many of them lighter in colour because of the mingling with Nordic blood from shipwrecked mariners, stood about the doors of their adobe huts hoping that we would talk to them. Giant cacti gave the rounded hills and the dry, open valleys the prickly look of avocado pears.

After making our official entry into Mexico (it is cheaper to do this here than in any other port in the country) we set sail across the mouth of the Gulf of California. The first night out we were, as so often happened, becalmed. There was little swell, the night was overcast and the stillness was intensified by the creaking of the mainsheet blocks as the mainsail, hauled in tight to prevent its slatting, tried in vain to free itself. Below us the inky water was alive. A huge manta ray glided by, its enormous fins, like the wings of a delta jet, outlined by the phosphorescent water; there were dolphin and porpoises, sea-snakes and a slim, good-looking young shark that rubbed himself for hours against our copper to our mutual advantage. A breeze sprang up from the south-west and landed us off the entrance to Mazatlan twenty-four hours later. Creston Island, shaped like a hound resting its head between its paws, plays the devil with the wind, and a backlash put us almost on top of a reef. Christopher jumped for the engine, Anne ran forward to back the jib, and another puff from the opposite direction, thank God, blew us off again.

A little later Christopher's worried face appeared at the hatch, "I can't get this damned engine to go," he said.

I had been so busy I had quite forgotten him.

In the port no one noticed our presence, so the next day we went along to the Port Captain's office. We waited an hour. He was a big man for a Mexican, his face hidden in rolls of fat, and a large cigar rotating between his lips. Our few formalities were soon concluded and we were about to leave when a clerk with padded shoulders and eyes as cold as granite whispered, "Dues for pilotage."

The Captain frowned, "This is an English yacht," he said.
"No matter," said Granite Eyes. "All ships must pay."

I waved my cruising permit in front of him but this he ignored.

He said, "That has nothing to do with us. At Mazatlan, all ships pay."

I said, "But we had no pilot."

"That makes no difference, Captain."

"How much do we owe?"

The Port Captain looked at our register. "Sixty-three pesos."

Granite Eyes took him up at once. "This yacht came in on Sunday. One hundred and twenty-six pesos for overtime."

I said, "How can there be overtime if no one comes out to our ship?"

Granite Eyes shrugged his shoulders. The heat of the noonday sun, the difficulty of understanding what they said made my head reel, but Anne looked cooler than ever. Her Spanish is basic.

She said, "Si conocer el reglemente aqui, Capitan, restamos un otra dia y noche al mar."

The Captain rose to his feet. He took his cigar from his mouth and bowed to her. "There has been a mistake." He glared at Granite Eyes in a way which made that very unpleasant young man grow paler still. "This yacht, this English yacht, came in today. I saw her myself." He turned to me. "That will be sixty-three pesos, Captain, thank you."

The town is very Spanish, with its streets dreamy and quiet during the hour of the siesta, the blue and gold cathedral, the glimpse through an open window of a child kneeling before an altar, for it wanted less than a fortnight to Christmas, and each little house had its shrine.

Behind and to the north is Indian country; hundreds of square miles, we were told, where the rites of the witch-doctors and the distilling of *peyotl* from the cactus root are still carried on much as they were in Cortez's time. If a white man strays too far he may be warned off and allowed to return or on the other hand he may disappear like D. H. Lawrence's *Woman that Rode Away.*

The season was now far advanced and any moment, they said, we could expect a brave north wind, but our luck was out and our slow progress down the coast continued. We put into Banderas Bay because, on our chart, there was a place with the name of Santa Cruz de Juan de Costello; such a place, we felt, ought to be worth a visit, but all we could see was a deserted lime-kiln, a dug-out canoe with a mast and sail, and two small huts. As we were learning fast, the poorer the community the more truly hospitable it is to the passing stranger. We were met by a deputation, and to our surprise a well-dressed young woman spoke to us in slow and urgent tones about a child whom she thought might be having pneumonia. On hearing that I was a doctor she hurried me away to an adobe hut with a few broken slats on the outer wall and a roof of thatch with a hole to let out the smoke from the fire. The child was wrapped in sacking, and I had to do as the French country doctors do, listen to the child's chest with my ear, an indignity to which the baby naturally objected in the strongest possible terms. Thanks to antibiotics, it made a quick recovery.

Señora Beatriz, who came from Mexico City, was staying with her brother Pedro round whose ranch the village revolved. His hut was larger than the others and was supported by a great brazil nut tree, which grew in the middle of the room. A stove built of lime had an ingenious device for making *tortillas* easily and an oven for cooking. Beatriz, her two young daughters, her brother and another young woman who may have been a sister, all lived in this room, but they did have beds which were frames of wood with rope netting (like our bowsprit shrouds) and supported at each end on empty oil-drums. The estate lay behind the village in a broad valley and here pumpkin, frijoles, callabasos, maize and trees of papayas grew. Loaded with papayas for our voyage Pedro chose for us an enormous pumpkin which he said would last for weeks. Beatriz, without a thought, whipped off her outer skirt, rolled it up into a small cushion, put it on her head and carried the pumpkin home.

As it grew dark I noticed that none of the peasants were

conscious. They lay about in a sort of stupor, and if one got in the way Pedro, not ungently, put him on one side like a child. Was this the result of *peyotl*, or an unusual reaction to alcohol? I should have liked to have asked him.

As there were no roads the products of the rancho had to go by sea to Puerta Vallerta, a place we had been warned against visiting because of the violent swell upon the beach. We saw the canoe sail that night. Her sail was mast-headed and her skipper, a young lad, wedged himself in between the sacks of maize and fruit. There could have been no more than six inches of freeboard by the time everything was in, and I was glad that the night was calm.

We put into Manzanillo for Christmas and were at sea for New Year's Eve, and how we longed for wind down that bare and arid coast. Off Cabo Corrientes a contrary current held us up for three days, and after that we changed our tactics, following the bays round at night, keeping close to the shore as Bill Phillips suggested we should.

Bill was one of those people who kept turning up in unexpected places. We had met him at Balboa in the ketch *Blue Peter*, and then he had dropped casually in to see us at the Royal Victoria Yacht Club having bicycled over from the Empress Hotel. We got to know him better still at San Diego where he lived. I think Bill was in the advertising business, but it was as an explorer and a cruising man that he was known among his friends. He knew the coast from San Diego to Panama better than most, and had once sailed his ship far up the Chiriqui River before taking a canoe into the interior where no white man had ever penetrated. The natives were unclothed and resembled those that Slocum described in his passage through the Magellan Straits. It was this, Bill said, that gave him the idea of modernizing Slocum's methods by using an electrified fence instead of the Captain's tin-tacks.

Bill's words to us were "Keep just outside the breakers." And I'm sure Bill was right, for more than once I remember going up the ratlines while the ship was slipping bravely through the water to find that a mile to seaward there was not so much as a ripple on the moonlit sea. Although we lived with the roar of the breakers in our ears night after night and week after week, I must confess that I felt the strain, for I am not one of those iron-nerved men who take such things philosophically. Even now on a quiet night in an Essex creek I can still hear those breakers.

A mile off-shore . . . those were the instructions; but the interpretation of what a mile might be was left to the watch. Mine, Anne used to say when she came up to peer at a rugged cliff, was definitely short and hers, I know, was long; while Christopher's (he was short-sighted) was a little uncertain. Before dawn on 3 January the loom from the lights of Acapulco showed up on the port bow, and in the morning we sailed past sheer precipices of rock with tiny houses hanging in the clefts, through the Boca Chica and into what must be one of the finest harbours in the world, like a sapphire set in a dark green bowl of hills. Bodies bronzing on the beach, old men paddling rafts with awnings to protect you from the sun, dark young men on skis twisting, jumping, turning behind foaming speed boats, smart yachts, coloured beach umbrellas, dance-bands, enormous hotels and the deep Mediterranean blue of the sky made one realize that Cannes or Acapulco, Honolulu or Blackpool, all are very much the same.

On land the tremendous noise and bustle in the market, the deserted streets behind, the little restaurant in a corner of a square belonging to two matadors (man and wife) great pans with lids that you lifted to inspect each dish simmering on the stove, the strumming of a guitar, the swirl of a flowing skirt, the clicking of the fingers, the swaying of a figure, all these brought back to us the earthy smell of Spain.

That flavour of Spain followed us when we took a bus inland; the dry hills, the peasants walking by the side of the road as the first light flooded the valleys, the two dusty little towns at which we stopped for refreshments, the thin, emaciated cattle, the goats on a high plateau and then at the end of the two-hundred-mile drive to the mountain town of Taxco, six thousand feet up, older than Mexico City itself, a fairy place with the twin brown towers of its Cathedral, the streets and houses straggling up a hill, the shady square on the brow, the shops filled with silver from the silver mines, and the advertisements for a bullfight to take place in the capital that week.

At Taxco we stayed with a Saxon baron and his wife who lived in Humboldt House. Their dining-room had been a Chinese Trading Post in 1593 where silks and spices from the Orient were stored when they were brought overland by mule-train from Acapulco, the port of disembarkation for the Manila galleons. The Baron, a friend of Count Von Luckner of *Seeadler* fame and an anti-Nazi, is an architect but is probably better known as an archaeologist, although he says that this is only his hobby.

His first wife was the great-niece of Franz Joseph, Archduke of Austria, whose murder at Sarajevo was the spark that kindled the first war. In the second war the feeling against Germany was so high in Mexico that when she was desperately ill at her last childbirth no doctor could be found to attend her and she died. Later the Baron married her niece, a tall slender girl with a sweet face. Between them they have eight children ranging from one year to seventeen. The passion with which they conducted their arguments in German, Spanish and English, and their flair for stage effect made me think I was watching a performance of *The Constant Nymph*.

The Baron was at that moment making a model of a tomb that he had found in which were the remains of the last Emperor of the Aztecs, Coatemo. Coatemo had surrendered the city of Mexico to Cortez, on condition that Cortez spared his life, only to be murdered by him shortly afterwards. The Aztec's family were most anxious that his body should be buried on sacred ground (for Coatemo was a Christian) and the priest who lived in his mother's village agreed to do this under a vow of secrecy. The secret was kept for four hundred years until, the last direct descendant having died, it passed into the hands of a distant cousin, the owner of a drugstore. He, after consulting the local priest, told the authorities in Mexico City, and they asked the Baron to investigate the story. He found no signs of the tomb beneath the church but discovered a record that the original church had been burned down and the present one built on top of it. Below the site of the original altar, and so well concealed that it took the Baron and his assistants weeks to unearth it, they came at last upon Coatemo. The emperor had had a fitting burial, for he lay in a hexagonal tomb surmounted by a dome and lacquered a deep red inside.

Our last port in Mexico was Puerto Angel, the Port of the Angel. Remembering our experiences at Mazatlan we trod delicately up the steps of the Port Captain's office, for we had failed to make our entry before noon that Saturday, and felt the threat of "overtime" hanging over our heads. The Port Captain was a jolly fellow. He greeted us warmly, showed us the view from his window looking over this enchanting bay, the Government wharf where a coaster called once a month, the winding path up to the scattered village, the fishing canoes drawn up on the beach, the whole place hushed and asleep in the afternoon sun.

He said, "It is good that you go now while there is no sign of one of those storms that come at this time of the year."

He gave us a clearance direct for the Canal Zone for which he charged us twenty-three pesos instead of the three hundred and sixty we should have had to pay for the same thing at Acapulco. He shook hands.

"Go tomorrow, while the weather is good. Buen viaje!"

But this place was so lovely that we could not tear ourselves away quite so easily. We shifted our berth to the other side of the bay where the sea whispered on a golden beach, and we spent one glorious day bathing and lying in the sun. A tiny lamp burned all night in a shrine in the burial ground which lay unobtrusively above our anchorage.

Puerto Angel is, however, a difficult place to lay in a stock of fresh food. The neighbouring town of Pochutla, said Claudia who did our washing, was *muy bien*, and her brother offered to take Christopher there by bus. They would be back, he said, by five o'clock.

By seven it was dark and there was no sign of Christopher, and I was just pulling the pram up to go ashore when I saw through the night glasses a small canoe approaching. Christopher and Glycerio tumbled aboard in the last stages of exhaustion: they had walked the ten miles back!

Pochutla, Christopher said, was a broken-down place like Corcubion in Spain. They had found little in the market, and Glycerio had gone from stall to stall muttering, "*Chyotes, no hay, papayas, no hay*," in evident distress. When they got back to the bus the driver was tired and would not leave for the port before morning.

Christopher had declined his companion's suggestion that he should wrap himself up in a *serape* and sleep in the street and had managed to goad him into walking home.

"I enjoyed my walk back," he said, "we had to wait to let two bulls finish a fight in the road, we met lines of *burros* each with its driver under impossible Mexican hats, a man with a string of iguanas hanging from his belt, two serpents, and a vulture picking at a dead dog."

CHAPTER TWENTY

THE TEHUANTEPECER

JUST as an American yacht bound for England would almost
certainly have heard of the Portland Race so had we been
warned of the Golfo de Tehuantepec before arriving in Mexico.
With barely concealed relish they told us of what had happened to coasters and steamers caught in a bad "Tehuantepecer" and of the yacht coming up the coast with a broken
tail-shaft which had taken twenty-eight days to sail across the
Gulf to Puerto Angel, and of how the water at the head of the
bay is forced out by the strength of the wind causing the current to flow in along both sides of the gulf at the rate of two
knots.

"The only way," they said, "is to follow the coast right
round, because, the wind being off shore, the sea is smooth."

With a powerful engine and with no sails set I am sure this
is the wisest course to pursue, but the risk of being dismasted by
the first onslaught of the gale if it arrived in the dark was too
great to take and as an ancient knight might walk delicately
across the mouth of the dragon's lair, so did we set off from
Puerto Angel with a light fair wind bound for the shores of
Guatemala three hundred miles away. As it grew dark, low,
flat clouds hid the darkening mountains, and the wind died.
The world was stilled.

In the tension of its coming the Tehuantepecer was like a
flying-bomb. At one o'clock in the morning a slow westerly
swell was the only sign of movement on the sea. When Anne
relieved me there was a light air from the north, and I went
forward to set the genoa, but in the short time it took me to do
this I noticed the ship was starting to pitch into a little swell
coming from the north-east.

An hour later Anne woke me. She said, "There's no wind to
speak of, but I'd like you to come and look at this sea."

I went up on deck. All around were seas with breaking
crests toppling aimlessly as if waiting for the wind to direct

Turtle soup and turtle steaks

Señor Contreras brought us the news
that Costa Rica had been at war with Nicaragua for a week

them. Only a whisper of a breeze filled our sails and the motion was like that of a toy boat in an agitated bath. On this occasion the wind came gradually; Force 3 to 4, Force 5 to 6, Force 6 to 7. Topsail and genoa had long since come down, and three reefs had been put in the main. Now, in the half-light of the dawn we pulled down the fourth and ran with the wind on the quarter. The sun came up like a ball of brass into a sky that was hard and white. The sea was becoming dangerous, and the wind was blowing a gale. We hove to and went below; all we could do was to wait. Of this waiting Anne wrote:

I am among wet pillows and blankets feeling seasick and unable to make Dramamine fight it. All day we lie in our bunks but get little sleep, and the wind and the sea throw us about. The motion is intense, the sea magnificent. Nothing is in sight, but we cannot see beyond our immediate wave, and Peter climbs the ratlines before dark with the riding light in case we should be blown across the steamer track during the night. I get out a tin of soup and one of corned beef but feel too sick so C. and P. deal with them, and later I sip half a basin of tepid asparagus soup with disaster. I rush to the hatch clutching my oily in my hand, just in time to hang my head over the top board. I go up after this unfortunate episode, and see a coil of rope has come adrift in the scuppers and go forward to see to it. Peter, who doesn't know I have left the after-deck, comes up and his voice is raised in a great cry: "*Where are you?*" All desolation was in those words, and I answer quickly and come down to lie again damply and suck a slice of pineapple.

About ten o'clock that night the whine of the wind rose several notes. Soon the mainsail would have to come down, as the ship was badly pressed at the top of every sea. For an hour we hung on till we could not bear the strain on hull and gear, even if *Moonie* could.

But, as we rolled out of our bunks, there was the faintest lessening of the wind. We stood huddled by the companionway half in and half out of our oilskins, and I thought how tired the others looked.

Slowly the wind came down the scale.

"Definitely less," we said, and turned into our bunks and slept.

11

By six o'clock that morning the wind had dropped to Force 6. I called the others without the slightest hesitation, for after the gale was over was the time when we must use the wind, for, according to Bill, the calm which follows a Tehuantepecer is only the precursor of another.

While they were shaking out some of the reefs I went up to take down the riding light. When I got to the hounds the motion was so violent I found that all I could do was to cling on with both hands and both feet. I let go the lashings, all but the last one, shouted to Christopher to man the spinnaker halyard, to which the head of the lamp was attached, and let go the last lashing. At that precise moment *Moonie* bucked like a mule and the lamp was torn from my fingers.

It flung itself against the mast, smashing the glass, swung forward and with long splinters like icicles hanging from a coping, it came straight for my head.

I caught it.

Glad that I was still alive and still aloft, and thinking that the seas would soon wash the blood from the decks, I guided it triumphantly below, to find that all this had not escaped the attention of the mate, but she was so angry that she forgot to ask me why I had not rigged a downhaul on it.

She said, "Where the hell d'you think you're going to get a new riding light!"

CHAPTER TWENTY-ONE

SIX COUNTRIES ALONG A COAST

TWENTY-FOUR hours later we were becalmed. The surface of
the ocean, which should have been as smooth as the Serpen-
tine on a summer's day, was wrinkled with tide-rips, and the
air was filled with a sibilant hiss as if thousands of sardines
were under way. This was not fish but current. The Tehuantepecer was over, and now all this sea was rushing back into the
middle of the gulf to replace the water which had been blown
out. It was an awe-inspiring thought.

The turtle was swimming towards us at about the same pace
as we were sailing towards him. Almost without thinking I
grabbed a gaff and hooked him under the armpit and hauled
him up the topsides. I called for help, for he weighed all of a
hundred pounds and Christopher left the helm and Anne
woke up. Remembering our shark in the South Pacific I
turned to Christopher:

"Get your gun and shoot him."

That turtle's innocent, almost trusting expression left a
memory that was only just surpassed by the excellence of his
steaks and the taste of his soup. After talking to a number of
ocean voyagers and reading the accounts of many others, it
seems that unless you live among the fish like the Norwegians
of *Kon-tiki* or Dr Bombard in his raft, catching them is a
chancy business. Only Anne refused to be defeated, and it
was not till we reached the shores of Mexico that her persis-
tence won. On one of those rare days when the sea breeze
attained Force 4 she threw the fishing-line overboard. That a
salmon plug, reminder of our unsuccessful British Columbian
days, was still attached to it did nothing to dismay her. She ran
it over a cleat on the boom to keep it away from the log line,
holding it in her hand. Suddenly I saw her stiffen, and without
a word she began to haul it in hand over hand.

Looking back along the ship's wake I saw the gleaming
under-body of an albacore swaying from side to side in a

163

despairing effort to escape. As well it might, for behind it there was something else.

"Oh, Peter . . . quick! There's a shark after my fish!"

Christopher came running up with a hammer, and between them they landed the albacore, cheating the shark, enraged at the sudden loss of his meal, by inches. From that day on, from the coast of Mexico to the Gulf of Panama, all we had to do if there was enough wind, was to stream the fishing-line at half past six to catch a fish for dinner.

Guatemala, whose mountains we sighted seven days after leaving Puerto Angel, has for its principal port the open road-stead of San Jose, but the sight of the breakers upon that beach frightened us off and we passed it by. The coast is low, and the mountains, nearly thirty miles away, look deceptively close, so that if you approach them, as we did, towards evening it is as well to know exactly where you are. And all down this rather featureless coast with its infrequent lights and uncertain currents, I fixed the ship's position by celestial navigation as a check to dead reckoning.

Almost without knowing it we had passed from sub-tropical Mexico into the lush jungle of the Tropics, the huts and little beehive dwellings of Indians replacing the compact little towns that we had occasionally seen along the shores of Mexico. Presently the plain gave way to foothills, the foothills to mountains. Many were cone shaped, but one, as we approached it with the aid of a fine sea breeze and more than a half knot of favourable current, seemed to have a cloud permanently above it. Rumblings like those from a distant thunderstorm grew louder, and soon there could be no doubt that one of these innocent peaks was erupting. We passed it at night. It looked like a flower-pot glowing with inner fires, and every now and then a river of molten lava would pour down the valley. I broke my rule about keeping a mile off shore and increased it to three, but the dry, rending sound of those sub-terranean explosions made it difficult to sleep, and once during Anne's watch a "red ball of fire like a trailing flare" fell into the water not far to the west of us.

With a fine offshore breeze we sailed past La Libertad in El

Salvador where *Tai-Mo-Shan* once lay. So bad was the surf that her crew, who wanted to visit the town of San Salvador, were taken off by a motor-boat and hoisted ashore by a crane. We passed it by, but the glare from the lights of a modern town, for that is how they speak of the place, two thousand feet up and in the middle of this wild and lonely country, struck us as a little odd.

Two days later we anchored off the Island of Meanguera in Fonseca Bay. Eleven days had passed since we had set foot on dry land; tantalizing when you are so near that you could almost jump on to it. We were within three miles of Amapala, and in the morning we went up on deck to see what sort of place it was. Anne wrote in her diary:

"The day is happy and alive with colour, yellow and gold flowers on the island astern, with its blown, dry trees and slashes of red and gold earth. On Conchaginta Island there is a bay and a little village. The sails of native boats glimmer in La Union channel, and a steamer lies off Amapala. We think we will sail up on the flood this afternoon."

But Anne was wrong. Christopher, buried deep in the fo'c'sle, was hunting cockroaches, I was trying to mend the riding light. The ship heeled suddenly and steeply; a bowl of dirty water catapulted, in company with a half decarbonized Primus and a tin of Vim, on to the starboard bunk. By the time we came on deck, it was blowing half a gale across seven miles of open water, and it would not be long before we started to drag towards the island.

How curious it is that, when every moment counts, one's mind has time, without impairing its efficiency, to turn back a page or two of memories, and I saw, quite clearly, the sea-wall at Muros Bay in Spain. That I had once again anchored in a place vulnerable to the only wind that was likely to blow with any violence seemed so criminally negligent that I dared not contemplate it, but Providence, aided by my crew, who without speaking a word, got sail upon the ship quicker than I would have believed possible, intervened and with twenty yards of grace, it looked no more, we sailed the anchor out and made an offing.

As we gybed and ran for the open sea Christopher, still a little out of breath, wailed, "Peter! Surely you're going to Amapala?"

"And miss this wind?" I exclaimed.

But I must confess, in all the hurry, I had forgotten the place!

Like the proverbial scalded cat, *Moonraker* raced out of the Gulf of Fonseca with the norther hard on her tail. The sun went down, and the moon came up, and the ship stormed along the dark and deserted coast of Nicaragua. At the change of watch I went up to relieve Christopher and saw to my astonishment the lights of a town fine on the port bow.

We had, up to this moment, been keeping two miles off shore to avoid Speck Reef but if this were Corinto, Speck Reef lay miles astern.

I studied the chart. It was possible, I supposed, that with the norther still blowing as hard as ever and the increased rate of current caused by the magnificent offshore breeze, this might indeed be Corinto for it seemed unlikely that a new town should have sprung up where the chart, corrected to two years earlier, showed not even the presence of a village. The place was nearly abeam; we could see no flashing light although, if it were weak, which was more than likely, it would be hard to see against this blaze of light. Instinctively I had been edging closer in while Christopher and Anne peered anxiously ahead.

Suddenly I heard Anne cry out. "Someone's flashing a light at us. There it is again! Two short and a long . . . Peter, you're too far in. *Get out!*"

And as the words died on her lips a roar filled the air. Less than fifty yards away a great sea had reared its noble head and broken upon Speck Reef!

No sooner had we passed this upstart place than the loom of Corinto's light was seen ahead.

For two days and two nights that norther blew. It was as heady as a new wine; the speed of the ship, the astonishing way in which the coast fled by, helped by the prodigious current, made me light-headed, daring me to chance my hand through the Murcielago Channel. My excuse to my crew, who

were frankly horrified, was that it would make it easier to
fetch Culebra Bay without a tack, as if one tack, or even two,
would make the slightest difference, a point they vainly made
in argument.

As we approached Cabo Elena, a long, narrow peninsula
jutting far out into the sea, I must admit that qualms of
conscience assailed me, for it was blowing Force 6, the ship
was pressed, and this remarkable coastline is forbidding in the
extreme. Off the Cape is a rock like Cleopatra's Needle and all
round were the rugged Bat Islands though which this passage
led.

"There can be no sea in there," I reassured myself, "and
therefore no danger."

We rounded the corner. It was like entering a witch's
cauldron. The wind tore down the hills and rebounded from
the other side, and in the middle was *Moonraker*, buffeted and
bruised like a mouse by an angry cat! A small incident, as is
any mouse in a cat's life. But if ever you come down this coast
don't go through the Murcielago Channel if a *Papagayo* is
blowing.

Out of the witch's cauldron, we streaked across the bay to
enter what the *Pilot* calls the "finest harbour in Central
America". But in all this vast natural basin there was only the
howl of a dog and a light gleaming yellowly from the top of a
small cliff.

We went ashore in the morning. As there was a slight swell
running we employed our usual technique, backing the pram
in stern first and, when I gave the word, the others jumped out
and pulled the pram (and me) up the beach. Unfortunately I
misjudged the depth, and to my surprise, and very much to
theirs, they disappeared below the water. Three men, swarthy
and cutlassed, were coming down the hill. With not even a
smile but with perfect old-world courtesy they greeted Anne
and Christopher as they came up.

Señor Contreras invited us up to his rancho, where brothers
and sisters, nephews and aunts, gathered on a low, cool
veranda. Hens and geese, dogs and pigs ran through the open
house: at the back a blaze of red bougainvillea, carts with

wooden wheels, a plough that would have looked old-fashioned to a Roman peasant, and a long flat stone with holes for gourds of water.

When Señor Contreras rode back from the nearest puebla where he'd gone to buy fruit and bread for us, he brought us the news that Costa Rica had been at war with Nicaragua for the past week!

Although we had sailed only eight hundred miles since we had last been ashore, the land being continuously in sight had made the mate less strict with water, and now we were running short. Our friends told us they had water to spare, and took us down through a banana grove to a stream, a stagnant pool covered with green slime, over which hovered a million flies. I was about to decline their kindly offer when they showed me a small circular hole through which welled comparatively clear water. This, they indicated, was *muy benito*. We filled our water-bags and carefully poured into each the right amount of Chlorox before taking them back to the ship. As none of us was any the worse, this speaks volumes for Chlorox.

The long straight coast down which we had been sailing for so long now changed its character. There had of course been something to watch; a bird of prey falling upon another bird, a manta ray, weighing a ton or more, leaping into the air to fall back with a splash that could be heard for a mile, a native village by a stream, a fishing boat on passage. But from Culebra to the Gulf of Panama, deep indentations like those of Nicoya and Dulce penetrate far inland.

Between Cabo Blanco and Punta Burica lightning played in the east, rain-filled clouds, the first for many months, cast their shadows upon the forests. We were chased all night by a thunderstorm. When I took over from Christopher at four o'clock the thing was gathering speed. I was running before a brisk wind with everything set, when I became aware of a noise like steam escaping from a safety valve. It grew louder and louder and nearer and nearer, and then I saw it; a column of water as high as the mast, swaying like the stem of a flower bowing to a gentle breeze, a thing of grace and form, travelling straight towards me.

I gybed all standing.

The water-spout passed harmlessly by, watched by my disgruntled crew, who seemed to think I'd gybed for the pleasure of waking them up.

At the coming of the day the Cordillera Salamanca (12,000 feet), remote and unchallenged, looked down upon me.

In Bahia Honda in the Republic of Panama (like a bowl with serrated edges and green with jungle) we towed a native and his canoe to the village. It gave us an *entrée* and we were given, as a great delicacy, *conejo*, an animal half-way between a rat and a rabbit, and much tougher, I imagine, than either, and long strings of dried *tortuga* which hung from our ratlines like streamers.

It was blowing a norther the day we left, and outside the shelter of the land the sea was rough and wet. On rounding the Pilar Del Sal (it was covered with bird droppings and the colour of the salt we keep our bacon in) at the southern end of Isla Cibaco, we saw the most enchanting bay. It was small, yet deep; it was protected from the north, with a wide and curving beach, the shape of a half-moon upon which sat a hundred pelicans. A stream cascaded down the hillside and its solitude was undisturbed by man. It beckoned to us, like Eve to Adam.

The norther blew itself out, and reluctantly we tore ourselves away from the diving pelicans and the bubbling stream to battle our way along that particularly unpleasant bit of coast between Cabo Mariata and Cabo Mala where the wind is always ahead and the current against you. Then we stood close-hauled across the Gulf of Panama, found the current running up the south-east shore, and anchored off the Balboa Yacht Club three months to the day after leaving San Diego.

CHAPTER TWENTY-TWO

AN ENCOUNTER
WITH THE QUITO SUENO BANK

To go through the Canal from the Pacific side was more difficult to arrange, and I made the bad mistake, urged on me by an acquaintance, of trying to arrange a tow with a banana-boat without the permission of the Chief Dispatcher. I am no good at concealing truth, and it took him less than a minute to discover it. His face looked pained and grim and he suggested the only way was to be towed by a Canal launch at the estimated cost of over a hundred pounds. Even when I said I thought Cape Horn might be cheaper there was no answering smile.

He said, "I shall have to report this to the Assistant Port Captain. Be here tomorrow at ten."

I brought Anne with me. The Captain, she discovered, had been born in Aalborg in the Limfjord and was a friend of Captain Petersen who had been so kind to us at Skagen when we had been run into by a Danish fishing boat. She produced a photograph of *Moonraker* taken in Moorea, and he delighted us by recognizing her at once for a west country fishing boat.

Then he turned to me. "They tell me you wanted to be towed through by a banana boat. You know that's against the rules?"

I said I did, but explained the smallness of our engine and the difficulty, of which he was fully aware, of beating through the Canal.

He smiled, "By the time you get down to the Magellan Straits it will be winter. I think we'd better relax the regulations."

He shook us by the hand. "Leave it to me," he said. "I'll fix it."

Our interest had been roused by a particularly fine vessel in Balboa anchorage. The *Chiriqui*, a famous ocean racer, which under her late owner had many fine passages including a voyage to Easter Island, had now been sold to someone at Los Angeles and was being delivered by an amateur crew. Although I never counted them all at once there must have been at least seven of them.

She left the day after we arrived with a fine fair wind, her engine going full blast and the sail covers on. That night she returned.

I rowed over and asked what had happened. Her mate said, "Only the dynamo. We'll fix that in a day or two."

Again she set out with the same fine breeze, but this time she came back under sail, neatly handled, and picked up her buoy. I rowed over. No one came to the side, but one of the crew threw over his shoulder, "The engine's packed up."

On the day before our "transit" she set out for the third time, and believe it or not, that evening there she was again. And what d'you think was the matter now? With a crew of seven aboard she had put back because the automatic pilot had gone wrong!

During our stay at this end of the Canal the *Faith*, an American ketch, came in. Larry and Babe, with their son Bill, were fellow members of the Seven Seas Cruising Association, and we had met at Acapulco. Like so many Americans, Larry had built his own boat in his spare time (she is thirty-six feet long and of generous beam) and her after end was a conglomeration of switches, dials and cables to control the various instruments, automatic pilot, radio telephones, fathometer, direction finder and power winch, without which, Larry maintained, no sensible man would put to sea.

Although *Faith* was a little down by the head due to extra fuel tanks for her powerful engine and the charging plant, protected by a wooden cover, on the foredeck, Larry did in fact use his sails more than you would have expected.

They, like us, had had their share of "northers" and calms while coming down the coast and it was during one of these calms that an American steamer stopped and hailed them, asking them if there was anything they wanted. At first they said, "No." But Babe had a brainwave. "Captain!" Babe's voice rang out loud and clear, "have you any ice-cream?"

"Sure we have," was the Captain's answer. "How much d'you want? A bucketful?"

So a bucket of ice-cream was handed down.

Then Babe, bless her, had another idea. "Captain!" she sang out, "if you meet an English sailboat with a green hull and a red mainsail, would you give her some ice-cream too?"

"O.K.!" called the captain, his voice a shade less enthusiastic, Babe admitted.

As at that time we were a week ahead of them we never met that steamer; but I could not help smiling at the thought of our surprise, and delight, if she had suddenly dumped upon our deck a gallon of ice-cream!

Wishing to see for themselves what the transit was like, the "Faiths" came aboard with the Pilot.

By an unavoidable chance we arrived at the lock at dead low water springs, and at the third locking of the day when the sluice operators were thirsting for their lunch and one could abandon all hope of the sluices being opened at anything but full pressure.

Now this, of course, being our second passage through the canal, I thought I knew what to expect. There were two springs, two bow lines, two stern lines and four motor-tyres along the starboard side and one of us with a roving commission to put a fifth at any point where he thought fit. As I glanced round at the Pilot's "Stand by, now," the ship seemed trussed as tightly as Gulliver had been by the Lilliputians; but the next moment proved me wrong. Fighting like a cat, *Moonraker* stretched herself several feet away from her protector (the banana-boat) and, with a sickening lurch, hurled herself at the bigger ship, the top of the bulwarks taking all the weight of the blow. If Larry hadn't whipped the spare fender in at the most dangerous place our bulwarks might have presented a very curious appearance. As we reached the top the Pilot mopped his brow—because of the heat, no doubt—and said, "I wouldn't have thought those bulwarks were all that strong." Nor, to be quite honest, would I.

Our day was not yet over. The banana-boat, as if incensed at having this upstart mongrel tied to her tail, chirrumped along at a good seven knots, and the wind across Gatun Lake blew at twenty-five knots in our teeth. Tired, wet and depressed still further by watching the seas breaking right over the breakwater, we secured our ship with her stern to a float and strolled over to the restaurant in search of a meal. The covered veranda, the people standing and sitting in groups or strolling on the dock, put Anne in mind of a crowd of passengers waiting at a station for a train that never comes. Our depression didn't last long. Roy and Carol Rice came over to

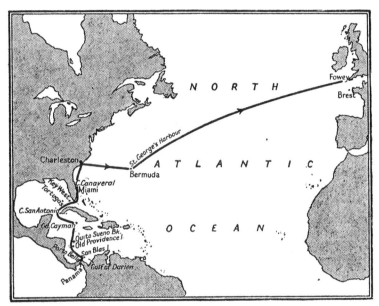

Panama to Fowey

our table bringing with them their guest. "Meet Peggy," they said.

Peggy was a compact little person with eyes that were very much alive. A journalist by profession, she had roamed the world; but the most remarkable thing about her (we got to know her well) was her ability to promote an aura of suppressed excitement wherever she happened to be.

Not so long ago she had bought a fifty-three-foot schooner

and sailed her from Florida through the Yucatan Channel to the Cayman Islands. As these islands are low and there was no one on board who could take sights, Peggy, not unnaturally, became anxious about her position. One of the crew, however, was a Cayman Islander and while Peggy was fussing with her charts (her words, not mine) he called her on deck.

"Captain!" he cried. "See those birds?" and Peggy looked up at a flock of birds that were flying off in different directions.

"Now, Captain," he said, pointing to each group in turn, "these are going to Grand Cayman . . . and those to Little Cayman . . . and those over there to Cayman Brac. Now bring me the chart and I'll show you where we are." As Peggy said, when they sighted the island the next morning, it was a perfect example of "position by triangulation of birds."

Her voyage continued: she had, she said, to leave Jamaica under a cloud and she had been in Old Providence Island only a week when a friend warned her that a gunboat had been dispatched from Colombia to order her arrest. I don't think for one moment that Peggy had done anything wrong; it was just that "authority" to Peggy was anathema, worse than a sea-lawyer to a bucko mate.

I, too, had made up my mind to sail by the Yucatan Channel and Peggy inspired us to call in at Old Providence; so on March 16, gilded with fresh paint and gleaming with varnish and resplendent in our new turkey-red mainsail straight from Sadlers at Burnham, we set sail in the evening and beat out of the incredibly narrow passage between the submarine nets guarding the entrance to the harbour and beat eastwards until Porto Bello lay abeam.

Carol Rice had told us that Porto Bello depressed her; nothing there, she said, but impenetrable jungle, buzzards, thin, ravenous dogs and tin shacks. But to us it had a different aspect; the old fortifications, destroyed by Drake and again by Morgan, still stand as grim reminders of those boisterous days, and the only way to reach the place is by the track the old mule trains used four hundred years ago across the Isthmus from Old Panama.

Near the site of the ancient church is the more recent one,

remarkable for the fact that it contains the image of the Black Christ. The image is striking. The figure, crowned by thorns, leans forward as if in anticipation of great events; the face is dark, the eyes piercing, and the wood of which it is made is almost black and *does not float*.

The story begins with the foundering of a Spanish galleon off the coast and the image being washed up on the shore. It was treated with great reverence, but three times it was pillaged, and on each occasion the marauding vessel sank and the image *floated* back into the harbour. A three-day festival is held every October to commemorate this astonishing legend.

The people, a mixture of Negro and Indian blood with a touch of Spanish here and there, were friendly enough and showed us their dummy turtles realistically executed in wood and stained to the right shade of brown with which they lured the genuine ones into the waiting trap.

For the rest Porto Bello is much as Carol described it, but it has a sheltered harbour, good holding ground, no swell and little sun, for along this coast there drifts a thin layer of vapour, giving it rather a sinister appearance which fits well the denseness of the jungle.

From here to the Gulf of Darien an easterly current, of which we were able to take full advantage, sets along the coast. We spent a night in the lee of Isla Grande that we might look across to where Drake lay . . .

> Slung atween the round shot in Nombre Dios Bay
> An' dreamin' arl the time o' Plymouth Hoe.

We hove to the next morning off the island of Porvenir. There are three hundred islets in the Gulf of San Blas, so that what we saw that morning were groups of palm trees scattered about the water, protected by long reefs, upon which the sea broke with an impressive roar. Indeed, so frightened was I of making a mistake, and not living to make another, that we ran back the way we'd come for a couple of miles to make absolutely certain of our position.

On this island of Porvenir, less than a mile long and a few hundred yards wide, lived the Acting Intendiente, Señor Hector Castillo; a youngish man with a cherubic face and humorous mouth turned down at the ends as if in ironic contemplation of his own misfortunes. Señor Castillo had broken his leg some years ago, and there was so much shortening that he was unable to walk a step without crutches, an accident, he feared, which would prevent him from ever rising in his profession.

He could now only look forward to ruling over several hundred islands inhabited here and there by small, long-haired men, dark brown in colour, whose women wore gold rings through their noses as a sign of individual wealth. The presence of two Panamanian sergeants, the Panamanian baker and his wife, the only woman on the island, only accentuated his isolation and increased his longing to return to his family in Panama on his yearly leave.

We dined with him that night, and our fellow guest was the captain of a copra schooner from Cartagena. I had wandered over to have a look at her as she lay against the primitive jetty. She was V-shaped, incredibly narrow, drew less than four feet and had no more freeboard than a long canoe. She was rigged as a gaff schooner with tall masts and on top of these they had fitted topmasts! She must go like the wind, I thought, but the seamanship to sail such a vessel in the rough winter seas of the Caribbean made me see myself as a very indifferent mariner.

The captain was a Colombian, soft of voice, a handsome man with the hallmark of a sailor. I had been able to do him some slight service in looking after one of his crew who had an abscess in the palm of his hand, for which he was quite unnecessarily grateful. I remember we talked about England, and I was amazed that in such a remote place they seemed to know exactly how our country was run (which is more than we do) and to follow the opinions of our statesmen as if the world's peace depended upon them. It was odd to us as Englishmen to find two men of different nationalities who thought so highly of our own.

We spent five days among the islands. Native huts with thatched roofs of palm fronds nestled under trees, and in some of the larger islands near the mainland, we were told, were communities living so equable a life that they could well be an example to other countries who might at first sight think themselves superior.

Rarely were we out of sight of a sailing *caraqua* off to the fishing grounds or to collect copra or to transport a family from one island to another. The San Blas Indians are a reticent people, nor could we understand a word of their dialect. They were as fierce in battle as they are at home on the sea, and a generation or two ago they defeated the Panamanian army that was sent to suppress them.

The evening before we left the shores of South America we dropped anchor in an enchanted bay of pale green water with foreshores of the palest sand, which, when you strode into the water for a swim, stirred up into a thick precipitate, like milk. I woke before dawn and rowed myself ashore, walking across to the windward side. In the growing light dark clouds came sweeping in from the sea on the wings of a fresh Trade Wind and from the barrier reef the ocean looked far from inviting. It suddenly occurred to me how far we were from England, a thought which might not have occurred if the wind had been reversed.

I was walking back to the pram trying to think of an excuse for delaying our departure when I thought of that Colombian copra schooner making her way back to Cartagena. Within an hour or two we were beating out of the channel on our way to Old Providence Island, a hundred miles off the east coast of Nicaragua and two hundred and seventy miles to windward.

Our voyage was blessed by good fortune; the North-East Trades were moderate to fresh and only for twenty-four hours did they blow hard enough to bring home how unpleasant the passage might have been.

Old Providence is a mountainous island which, like those of the Societies, has a reef extending some distance from the coast, enclosing lagoons of quiet water and with passes in and out. It is said to have been inhabited by Morgan's buccaneers, and its inhabitants now claim this distinction with the pride we all feel in our forbears if only they are bad enough. The island belonged to Great Britain, but Queen Victoria gave it away to

12

Colombia, an action that made the island violently pro-British. Indeed, when we anchored off a tiny village and broke out the Blue Ensign (a flag they'd never seen but whose nationality they guessed by the Union Jack in the corner), the coloured people came out in boats bringing presents of oranges, white bread and coconuts.

The clean, bracing air, the lovely wind, the jib-headed fishing boats, as crazy as those of Barbados, brought back to us the smell of the West Indies. I was out of action at that time, running a temperature and with an ankle so swollen and painful that I could not put my foot to the ground, but I enjoyed the sail to Catalina Harbour sitting on the foredeck with my leg propped up while Christopher and Anne did all the work, their faces instead of mine frowning in concentration over the pilotage.

A mile or so from our destination a native boat roared down under a press of sail.

"Captain, we pilot yo' into de harbour . . . very dangerous . . . ten dollars."

Ten dollars! Did they think we were flying the Stars and Stripes?

"Five dollars, then."

But Anne shook her head, and side by side the boats sailed along.

"Captain, if yo' won't take de pilot, we'll race you!"

Much to their astonishment, and to ours, we beat them to it handsomely.

The Port doctor was a Turk, educated in Colombia. He had a look at my ankle and suggested cortisone. I had been used in American to seeing this rather dangerous stuff handed out like aspirin, and I concurred. I think it did my ankle quite a lot of good, but it woke my duodenum up to such an extent that the discomfort accompanied me back across the Atlantic to the shores of England. And the doctor was not even qualified!

Ashore, the island is a curious mixture of English and Spanish; English spoken in the streets and stores, but when the sun goes down Spanish sung to a guitar instead of negro songs to a Calypso band.

Our friends the Faiths came in, and a few days later we sailed in company for the Quito Sueno Bank. This reef runs north and south for twenty miles, submerged along its entire length except for the last hundred yards, upon which has been built a light tower with a weak light (unwatched).

In the centre, on the leeward side, are two underwater crops of coral heads running to the westward for six miles and in between these, for those who could find it, was a sheltered anchorage. There we could lie out in the middle of the ocean with nothing but water to look at and no sound but the cry of a passing bird.

Now we made it quite clear, Larry and I, that we wouldn't attempt it in the dark. About five in the afternoon Larry came close alongside:

"Peter," he shouted. "D'you think it's safe?"

And I replied, "No, it's too risky."

So Larry started his powerful engine and drew ahead on his course for Jamaica. When he was safely out of sight we tacked towards where we thought the southern end of the reef might be.

It grew dark before we got there and, as I sat up on the crosstrees staring ahead I was reminded of that time five years ago when I tried to find Hogsty Reef at the same time of day. I had had the feeling, as I had now, that I was playing a dangerous game and that the only prudent thing was to clear out. But I didn't.

Anne and I were below finishing our dinner when Christopher called out, "Peter! What about those rocks you were worrying about?"

"We've passed them some time ago," I replied.

And at that moment she struck!

CHAPTER TWENTY-THREE

THROUGH THE STRAIT OF FLORIDA

THE impact knocked *Moonraker* over on to the other tack, and in a scene of the utmost confusion we dropped anchor on the first patch of sand that we could see, shimmering palely in the moonlight.

Ten minutes later the bilges were still dry. We lay all night to the full scope of our chain, and the drone of the wind and the chop of the sea seemed to emphasize the precariousness of our position. I slept little.

At first light Christopher went down with his underwater goggles and reported that the copper was torn in four places and that in at least one the wood was badly scored. As the sun rose higher we could see the fantastic growths coming up from the bottom, some thick and tough, others not so strong. Our coral head must have been one of the slender kind and broken off at the impact. We winched in the chain and under shortened sail we wove our way by eye through this prickly maze. We set course for the island of Grand Cayman three hundred miles to the north.

I was on watch when we expected to make our landfall, soon after dawn on the third day out. It was still dark, the moon was high, the sea smooth and the topsail had already been taken down to prevent a premature arrival off this low and ill-lit southern shore. Suddenly, something like panic overtook me; I became quite sure that land was dead ahead and at no great distance.

Leaving the ship to sail herself I climbed the ratlines and peered through the night glasses. No dark line appeared ahead, no smell of land, no sound of breakers. I checked the log; only the current was in doubt. Still with this sense of danger ringing in my head, I got the jib off her and was about to heave to, when I caught sight of a glow no bigger than a man's cigarette *broad on the port bow*! The Light! The current must indeed have been doing overtime. A small incident, but one that illustrates how unreliable moonlight is; that shore for which I had been so diligently searching could not have been more than half a mile away.

It was broad daylight when I worked the ship into George-town Bay, shaped like a wide V with the little town at its apex. To port was a white coral beach; and water, sky and land dazzled the cold eyes of a northerner with the intensity of light. The place was an open anchorage with a bad reputation for north-westerly winds. Speed was the thing if anything was to be done to *Moonraker*; and this was Easter Sunday.

Scarcely had we stowed the sails when a motor-boat put out from the shore. Papers. . . ? We showed our clearance from the Canal to Port Everglades in Florida, and in a moment official business was over. Was there anything, the harbour master asked, that he could do for us?

There was indeed; we were towed towards the shore through a narrow passage between rocks into a pool with a bottom of fine sand. Here we were made fast to half a dozen rocks. The ship was careened as far over as she would go, and within an hour "underwater shipwrights" (our term for men who ham-mer nails in under water) were working on the hull, en-couraged, no doubt, by the singing of hymns across the road from the House of God. They reported the planks to be badly scored, that in two places the wood had been penetrated to an unspecified depth, but that copper tingles should prevent the ship from leaking.

By four o'clock that afternoon, she was anchored off.

That evening a swell, slight but enough to have made such an operation as this quite impossible, rolled into the bay and did not cease while we were there.

The island is windswept, reminding us of Inagua in the Bahamas. There are houses without roofs, houses with only one wall still standing, evidence of the fearful hurricanes which have in the past devastated this low-lying land and drowned so many of its population. The Cayman islanders, as you might expect, are a race of seamen. As soon as a boy is old enough he will leave the land and ship aboard a turtle schooner or one of the deep-sea fishing-boats that work off the coast of Cuba.

We paid a call on Captain Benny Boden to whom we had an introduction from Bridget and Tony Reeves. When we arrived, the Captain, his wife, daughter and son, were busy sewing a huge expanse of canvas that would one day be *Yankee's* staysail. Anne, our sailmaker, had brought along the genoa which, in a Force 3 wind, had split from luff to leech, for it was as rotten as a pear. She asked the Captain, with a glance at me to silence any protest, how long it would take to make a new one.

The Captain asked, "When are you leaving?"

"Tomorrow," I said.

"Give me another day and I'll have it ready."

They finished that sail in less than the promised time and for half its cost in England.

The Trade Wind had settled in the south-east, and it was a topsail and spinnaker run to Cape San Antonio. We picked up the low hills of Cuba in the morning of the fourth day out, and late that night (so strong was the current against us) we were once more pitching into a steep sea heading for the Gulf of Mexico. I had wanted to explore the waters enclosed by the numerous cays that line the north-west coast of Cuba but having been warned at Grand Cayman that several fishing boats had been fired upon when approaching this coast we decided to keep the sea.

At dawn a cry of, "Sail on the starboard bow!" brought me on deck to find a Cuban schooner, a rakish-looking craft with the name of *Domingo Despues* (Next Sunday) bearing down upon us. She was almost bare of paint, her foresail a thing of patches, and her crew, dark and swarthy or as black as pitch, of the kind that might well have raised the Jolly Roger a century ago. Without a wave of the hand they circled us twice and then with vociferous shouts beckoned us to turn and follow them into some hole in the wall of Cuba. We declined their invitation and watched them disappear to the south-west with a feeling of relief.

Against a short, steep sea, and with a fine current, growing stronger every day, we pitched our way to the Dry Tortugas; but from Key West to Fowey Rocks we were rarely out of sight of the tall buildings and huge oil storage tanks that now deface what must at one time have been a paradise of islands. As we worked to the eastward the wind fell light and veered to the south, and the stream began to race.

I said, "We'll get to Port Everglades in the middle of the night. Let's anchor behind Fowey Rocks."

"There's no anchorage there," said Anne.

"If you go here . . . and here . . . and in behind that bank you'll be able to lie in comfort," I told her.

Christopher chewed his nails.

"As on Quito Sueno Bank, I suppose?" he said.

The low coastline slipped past at the rate of knots, and, marked by a haze of heat, the skyscrapers of Miami appeared to port like giant liners in a mist. We anchored off Miami Beach.

The dark sea, the gently rolling ship, the red, green and mauve neon lights lining the waterfront, the lighted windows reaching up to the stars and the roar of the traffic: it was all very exciting, as if you were sitting in the stalls watching a ballet (the dancing lights) illustrating the Tower of Babel.

In the grey light of dawn Miami took on that used look of a proscenium after the show was over, and we hurried on to Port Everglades to "clear" for the U.S.A.

From Port Everglades to Bahia Mar is a distance of about two miles, along the Intercoastal Waterway. We set off under sail, avoiding the innumerable power boats that dashed at speed in a north and south direction. It was rather like driving a farm cart across Piccadilly regardless of the traffic lights, and by the time we got there we were hot, exhausted and more than a little dishevelled. I am, however, an opportunist and I quickly pointed out to my crew who, for different reasons, wanted to sail to Charleston by the waterway instead of taking the outside route, that this would prolong our voyage for another year and probably for ever. Without a single word of protest, they agreed.

I don't know how many millions of dollars the Americans have spent on Bahia Mar Marina, but they are not a race to do things by halves, and there is everything here that the heart of an American yachtsman can desire: stores, Post Office, swimming-pool, bars, restaurant, dance bands and a glossy ship-chandler's that outshines Captain O. M. Watts's.

It was not the sort of place you would expect to find the Hiscocks or ourselves, but we had come here to see Ann Davison, about whom we had heard and read so much (she was the first woman to cross the Atlantic single-handed).

There is a quality about men and women who sail the high seas that is hard to define and even to detect if you meet them ashore, but the moment they come aboard they seem to fit into the atmosphere of the ship as if they belonged; nothing obtrudes, nothing jars. So it was with Ann Davison. "Steadiness" is the word I think I want to describe her presence.

The day before we were due to leave we were looking out over the Canal, when round the corner came a rather battered-looking ketch in search of a night's rest. Suddenly one of her crew waved vigorously in our direction, and then we recognized her. She was the *Zaira* and we had first met her at San Diego more than five months ago.

Zaira had left San Diego Yacht Club on her way to New York the day after we arrived there. She was spick and span, her spars shone with varnish and her crew, large and tough, were justly proud of her. She must have been about the same length as *Faith* but of narrower beam, she was bermudian-rigged on both masts, and had an echo sounder, an automatic pilot, a radio-telephone, a large and powerful engine and a charging plant. She was, in a word, well-found and looked a fast vessel. Before they left, we met her owner; rather small for an American, with bright blue eyes, a freckled skin, red hair and a chin like the Cabo de Roca. Passing the time of day I said we hoped to be in Acapulco for Christmas, but by then, he said, they would be in Panama as he had to get to New York in the spring.

To our surprise we saw her the moment we got to Acapulco. They had, the owner said, run into trouble at Mazatlan, had escaped to Manzanillo where they were hauled before the authorities, but had been rescued by an understanding Port Captain. This had meant delay and frustration, and the crew had left the ship as soon as she put into Acapulco. Now he was searching for another and soon after we left he signed on Olie Hall. Hall was a wiry South African who had the reputation of being a tremendous worker. He had come out with the Warrs in the *Muriel Stevens* from Capetown and was looking for just such an opportunity. They set off immediately, put into Corinto in Nicaragua for petrol and were charged a hundred and fifty dollars for harbour dues alone. They passed through the Canal ahead of us and had left Cristobal the day we arrived there.

Their passage to Jamaica had not been an easy one. The wind had risen to gale force and they had been driven through the channel between Rosalind and Mosquito banks and had even sighted Cape San Antonio, over four hundred miles to leeward of their destination.

Nor was this all. Their sails blew out, two main halyards parted, and the three of them, for the owner's young brother had joined them in Panama, sewed sails day and night. Then the ship started to leak. The engine packed up, the charging plant was flooded, no lights, no echo-sounder, no ship-to-shore telephone, no automatic pilot. There must have been times, with the water over the cabin sole, when it might have seemed wiser to run down wind to the nearest port, but this did not seem to occur to the owner. He said he was going to Jamaica and to Jamaica he went. It must have been something to do with that chin!

From Jamaica they sailed through the windward passage, and while they were close-hauled under the lee of the land they went ashore on Crooked Island very near the place where the *Tai-Mo-Shan* stranded. After three back-breaking days of hard work they got her off without help and reached Nassau, where they were at last able to get the engine repaired; and now they were here on their way to New York.

The owner looked at *Moonraker* with a rueful grin. "You might think, Doc., that this was a case of the tortoise and the hare!"

CHAPTER TWENTY-FOUR

THE LAST DITCH

HOPING for a fast passage with a fair wind and the Gulf Stream under us we set off for Charleston four hundred miles to the north. It was not exactly a coastwise passage, for north of Cape Canaveral the land trends to the west of north, forming a great bay a hundred miles deep between here and Hatteras.

In the afternoon a thunderstorm of great intensity gathered over the land and over the seas astern. Flashes of lightning, peals of thunder and torn clouds travelling at great speed made us take the topsail down, but nothing more came to us than a fresh breeze. Later, a heavy northerly swell came rolling down from the wastes of the North Atlantic.

Followed four days of head winds, thunderstorms, gusts of nearly gale force and the filthiest sea (the current being against the wind) that I have ever tried to drive a boat to windward in.

The rest of the voyage was uneventful, and on the seventh morning out the coastline south of Charleston was in sight. With a fine fair wind and a sluicing tide we roared through the narrow entrance leaving the mellowed buildings, the cannon on the Battery and the slender spire by Wren to starboard and entered the Intercoastal Waterway to find a berth in Wappoo Basin, a muddy creek where tiers of elderly boats are made fast to wooden stages with rotting posts.

I can think of no better American landfall than Charleston for an Englishman; the quiet houses with walled gardens, the air of leisure, the sense of the importance of the past.

Hardly had we secured our ship to the posts when a girl came out of the office of the small boatyard and summoned me to the telephone.

"Hurry," she said, "they're calling you from New York State." Over the wire, as clear as if she were speaking in the same room, I heard Bee Hodge's voice (Bee was a friend we'd met in Lauderdale).

"Peter! Are you all right?"

"Why, of course."

"But that thunderstorm on the day you left. Didn't you get caught in that?"

And when I explained that it had passed harmlessly astern, she continued, "That storm did two million dollars' worth of damage at Fort Lauderdale and they had winds of a hundred and twenty miles an hour at the airport."

As I walked back to the ship it seemed to me that the times that Providence had intervened were mounting up.

Christopher went off to stay with friends at Greenville while friends of ours from North Carolina came down to take us back to Fuquay Springs.

They drove us through the Smokey Mountains and we spent a Sunday at Chapel Hill. The orchestra playing on the campus, the attentive audience in a circle on the grass, the tall trees, the red brick college buildings in the distance, the quiet little town under the hot Carolina sun: the South, little different from that of Scarlett O'Hara.

On the way back our friends drove us to Fayetteville to catch the Atlantic Coast Express. I had stupidly misread the time-table and we arrived one minute before the train was due to draw out. Leaving the others to carry a mountain of gear (Anne and I take as much for a fortnight as most people do for a year) I raced on to the platform and went straight to the "fountain head".

Panting, I said, "Look, we've *got* to catch this train. Can you wait?"

To which the driver, leaning down from the cab of the enormous diesel-electric locomotive, replied, "O.K. I can hold her."

In all the bustle of getting aboard, I still had time to wonder what would happen if an American, vivid in a shirt of many colours, rushed up the platform at Paddington and tried to stop the Cornish Riviera Express.

Out of the wide estuary and between the stone breakwaters where the hustling seas, sharp and prickly with tide-rips make *Moonie* watch her step, out through the buoyed channel beyond which they break in anger on the shallow sands and into the wide Atlantic where the wind, now unfettered, falls light and leaves us time to contemplate our departure from the Promised Land.

How can we give a proper impression of so vast a continent from six months' sailing round her coasts, or an unbiased one when we are leaving so many friends behind us? But, as you were so insistent, Carol, I will try.

Your country glitters and you forget, being used to all these brassy lights, that our eyes are not accustomed to it and you forget, or perhaps you have never realized, that we English are so very different, a difference that is made more difficult to understand by having a common language; although you are doing your best to remedy that defect. Englishmen as a race are what you call in America, "sales-resistant". If you come to our country, which I hope you will, no Britisher will try and "sell" it you, because his love for it is deep. He will grumble at its fogs, its climate, its taxes, its government and almost anything, except perhaps, the English spring.

And when he returns your visit he may be embarrassed by the enthusiasm of your welcome and unable to swallow America when you push it down his throat. He may go even further and think you are trying to persuade yourselves that you are "God's Own Country" because in your hearts you have your doubts about it. May I make a suggestion?

Let him open his eyes on it and absorb it for a little and then he, like us, will go back to Britain and tell his friends that you are indeed as fabulous as you think you are.

It is rather less than eight hundred miles from Charleston to Bermuda. On the eighth day out the glass was falling, the weather threatening, and there was no chance of getting a sight. Dark before its time, the night came on, and I was reminded of Ed Ayres's remark made to me five years ago when leaving Ponce de Leon Inlet.

"Good sailing to Bermuda," he had said, "if you can find it."

We should, if my reckoning was right, have sighted land an hour ago. The three of us on deck, the rain, long foretold, slanting down; the ship under shortened sail; how long could

I safely carry on? Better be sure than sorry, on such a night
. . . and then Christopher's great shout:

"Peter! Quick! The Light; right above you!"

Like a street-lamp in a London mist, Gibb's Hill Light
flashed out.

It is a wise skipper that never lets a fair wind run to waste.
Day after day it blew fresh from the west while I fretted in
St. George's Harbour; but Christopher had never been to the
island, and we had friends to see again. Five days went by
before we let go our lines and sailed through the Town Cut
bound for Fowey in Cornwall.

Three hundred miles later I was at the helm. It was a blue,
sparkling day, Christopher and Anne were asleep in the cabin,
and I was easing the old ship over a cross swell which at times
made her roll the last two feet of her boom under the crest of a
sea. My mind, except for watching the swell, was a thousand
miles away, when suddenly, right out in the middle of this
great sea, there was a crash!

I was amused at the bewilderment and alarm in Christopher's face as it appeared in the hatchway, because it must so
closely have mirrored my own. Both he and Anne thought the
mast was coming down, and I that the bottom was falling out!

Three chastened mariners, a broken bobstay-tackle, a bent
stem-plate, a thrashing tail a few feet from our planking, green
slime spreading like oil upon the waters, marked the end of this
encounter.

Perhaps it was as well; for the whale cleaned off our barnacles and we cleaned up the whale.

I was interested, some months later, to hear Peter Scott, in a
broadcast, say that whales are soft. Soft is a relative word.

The days passed pleasantly enough. We crossed the broad
band of the Gulf Stream, and once we had left it to the south
we had real passage-making weather, the stuff I'd dreamed
about down the windless coast of Mexico. Our hopes were high
and our spirits soared, a hundred and forty-five miles on the
clock; and then came a change. The glass fell, and great black
clouds hung menacingly astern.

In the middle of the night, Anne recorded, they decided to

advance. Long flashes of forked lightning, thunder and torrential rain, calms and catspaws kept her standing there "like
a patient cow in a rain-soaked field". Right in the middle of all
that blackness she suddenly saw a star, as if nailed to the masthead. Puzzled, she altered course wishing to throw it off, but
the star, now more like a thin bar of fire, kept wandering up
and down the top three feet of mast. Softly she called me, but
I was sound asleep and Christopher (who was very wide
awake) went up instead. "Good heavens," he exclaimed,
"you've caught St. Elmo's fire."

After the last peal of thunder, the last vivid flash of lightning,
the last squall, all the wind, so it seemed to us, vanished from
the face of the North Atlantic. My log, of course, does not con-
firm this.

There were periods of calm lasting twelve hours or more,
there were days when the wind, mostly ahead, reached Force
1 to 2, but there were others when we ran before a gentle
breeze, and once we covered a hundred miles. Christopher
became more like a shaggy dog than ever, his trusting eyes
resting upon me confidently to find a breeze from somewhere,
myself irritable and cross partly because I still cannot take
calms equably, and partly on account of the effect of the cortisone the Turkish doctor gave me; while Anne wrote:

"I don't feel as if I ever lived anywhere but on the sea, and
the days go by all too quickly, even the damp and misty ones."

The S.S. *Gardenia* of South Shields (looking like Masefield's
poem) steamed sedately by; a happy ship, we thought, and her
north country skipper paid me the compliment of not giving
me her position. The S.S. *Empire Merchant*, on the other hand,
left us alarmed and despondent for we disagreed by a whole
degree of longitude!

It took me the rest of the day to make sure that this had been
due to our mis-hearing, for at that time I had been thirteen
days without a time signal.

One night the ship was becalmed, and I noticed the masthead lights of a steamer in line a long way astern of us; but
steamers move fast these days. I once met a man, an Englishman, who had found himself as lighthouse-keeper on Race

Rocks which, you may remember, is a focal point to traffic coming up the Juan de Fuca Strait. Before dawn on a February morning he noticed the masthead lights of a steamer dead in line coming up the Strait, about five miles away. The weather was clear and the sea was smooth. My friend, who had the instincts of a seaman, kept his weather eye lifting and when the steamer was less than a mile away he suddenly realized that she had not yet seen the light and was heading straight for disaster. Fortunately, he and his colleague had been overhauling the fog-signal the previous evening and the airtanks for starting the fog-horn engine were full. He blew him a U. Two short blasts and a long. You can imagine that skipper's feelings. It must, to him, have sounded like the trump of doom. The steamer, steaming at fifteen knots and helped by a strong flood-tide, heeled violently to starboard, passing *inside* a buoy that was anchored on a reef.

These masthead lights were rapidly getting nearer and it seemed to me that if a brand-new steamer of a well-run line could not see the light from a tower eighty-six feet high, this one might well not be able to see me.

Quietly, so as not to wake the others. I started the engine, and not till the ship's red light glowed at me unwinkingly did I stop it again.

Five hundred miles from Fowey the wind came in from the north-east. As the weather was pleasant our progress, though slow, was not too disagreeable. We crawled over the banks which lie across the mouth of the English Channel, and here it blew hard for a day, forcing us towards the French coast. Brest lay temptingly close, but what, after all, did a few days matter? The wind, seeing that it could not now deflect us from our purpose, kindly backed to north.

We picked up the Lizard Light as it winked out at the beginning of the night, twisted our way through two lines of steamers and in the early morning of the fortieth day out from Bermuda, lay becalmed three miles from the Dodman.

The sun soaked up the haze, and the town of Fowey was just out of sight. In an hour or two, or three or four, a breeze would come and we should sail in through the Heads into the harbour from which we had set out three years ago. What changes should we find, I wondered, and how should we take to living on the land? Would Christopher pad about the city in bare feet and a bowler hat, and should we be content with creeks?

My thoughts were disturbed by the sound of a vessel's engine and a boat came up that was familiar. She stopped, her sails casting their shadows upon the water. Her people welcomed us.

"Come aboard," I said, "and have some coffee."

And I hurried down to start the Primus.

Presently Anne looked out.

"Hullo," she said, "where have they gone to?"

"They wanted to get in," said Christopher. "They've already been two nights at sea."